THE TOP 10 LEADERSHIP CONVERSATIONS IN THE BIBLE

STEVE MOORE

Published by **nexLeaDeR**

Published in Atlanta, Georgia, by nexleader foundation in associa-tion with BibleCenteredLeadership.com.

ISBN: 978-0-9993508-0-5

Library of Congress Control Number 2017913176

Printed in the United States of America

What people are saying about...

The Top 10 Leadership Conversations in the Bible

"Steve Moore is not just a former student, he is an engaged practitioner and motivated promoter of many of the key concepts I taught at Fuller Seminary. Steve has become a champion of my work on Bible Centered leadership, and I've passed the baton to him with my blessing as it relates to this ambitious project. Heed Steve's advice and you will be blessed."

Dr. J. Robert Clinton, Professor Emeritus of Leadership, Fuller Theological Seminary, School of Intercultural Studies

"There are lots of leadership books but nothing quite like *The Top 10 Leadership Conversations in the Bible*, by Steve Moore. Practical. Positive. Interesting. Biblical. Well written. Read it like a bestselling management text, like a biblical exegesis or like a page out of your own leadership journal—this book combines them all and more."

Leith Anderson, president, National Association of Evangelicals

"This is a book on leadership like no other. It is in a category all by itself. This is not just opinion but new in-depth research on Biblical leaders and their conversations which results in basic principles to practice. This has never been done before. Reading chapter 00 is so captivating that the reader is absolutely compelled to continue. The opportunities to access the book span the range from the digital immigrant to the digital native. I believe it is a catalytic book that will be reshaping leadership for the common good now and in the future."

Jo Anne Lyon, Ambassador, General Superintendent Emerita, The Wesleyan Church

"I've been excited about my friend Steve Moore's new project from the first time he talked about it with me. I have a "top 10" brand of my own and love the concept of *The Top 10 Leadership Conversations in the Bible*. I believe this book and companion web site will help advance the cause of Bible Centered leadership."

Hans Finzel, president of HDLeaders, bestselling leadership author

"After 20 years of leading a leadership development ministry, I believe everything valuable that we can learn about leadership, has its roots in the Bible. That is why I'm so thankful for the research Steve Moore has done in this book about leadership conversations in the Bible. I've known Steve for more than a decade and I'm encouraged by his commitment to champion the cause of Bible centered leadership."

Jane Overstreet, president, Development Associates International

"I have a firm belief that everything we do should be rooted in the Bible. As a student of leadership, I am truly blessed by this research and well written contribution by my good friend, Steve Moore. I am sure that it will be of great benefit to the global Body of Christ as it is so anchored in the narrative of the Scriptures. Whether you are a local church leader, a ministry leader or an organizational leader, lessons learnt in this book will add great value to your life and leadership competency."

Peter Tarantal, Associate international director: OM and chair of WEAMC

"I invited Steve Moore to teach a leadership lesson to the ministry staff at 12Stone Church on Bible Centered Leadership. When I heard more about the research he was doing on leadership conversations in the Bible I knew this needed to become a book. The added component of the searchable database on the web site takes this to a whole new level! I highly recommend this valuable resource to any serious student of leadership."

Dan Reiland, Executive Pastor, 12Stone Church

"Steve Moore didn't have to convince me that the Bible is loaded with leadership lessons. I believe that with all my heart and have taught others so for a long time. Even so, reading this book—which, by the way, I found very hard to put down—has made my heart burn anew with a passion to introduce others to the Bible's profound leadership insights and train them how to drink deeply of the Scriptures as a lifelong leadership wellspring. I plan to share it and soak up its wisdom together with my students and colleagues."

Ralph Enlow, president, Association for Biblical Higher Education

"There are few people I know who ask the depth of questions and have the willingness and courage to apply what they have learned, regardless of the level of disruption, as Steve Moore. So, in this book we are not getting some theory Steve has picked up and written down, rather, we have the privilege of journeying with him through these biblical examples, gleaning valuable insights from his understanding and leadership journey. Whether you are stepping out in leadership or have many years under your belt this book will be incredibly relevant, challenging and inspiring."

Andrew Scott, CEO, OM USA, Author of *Scatter*

"If you read only one book on leadership I urge you to make it this book. Steve Moore will take you on a different kind of leadership journey. It will be enduring because it is marked by patience—no quick ix but rather a long season lingering with God and the Scripture. It is founded on humility—a willingness to learn from any person and any circumstance through which God chooses to speak. You will be led by a coach whose own leadership soul has been formed by these things and many more he will share."

Scott Arbeiter, president, World Relief

"Providing fresh insight, inspiring perspective, and profound leadership equipping straight from scripture is Steve Moore's forte! Three decades of close relationship has allowed me to repeatedly witness Steve's remarkable skill to mine God's Word for the absolute highest and best means of doing leadership God's way. His life-long devotion to pass spiritual and leadership wealth on to others makes him a sought after speaker, leader, consultant, and gifted author of this must-read book for all aspiring, spiritually motivated, and seasoned Christian leaders!"

Dr. Dwight Robertson, Founder/CEO - FORGE-Kingdom Building Ministries, Author of *You are God's Plan A...and There is No Plan B*

"Steve Moore has dedicated his life to the issues of leadership development through his research, writing, and exemplary life. I consider The Top 10 Leadership Conversations in the Bible to be his greatest gift to the Christian community! His thorough biblical research, stories from the Scriptures and Christian history, and personal insights all combine to provide a resource for personal encouragement and leadership training. For every Christian leader – from young beginner to seasoned veteran – this book is a must-read."

Paul Borthwick, senior consultant, Development Associates International

"Steve Moore has distilled ten important concepts that every one of us in leadership must consider. As I read this book I was forced to stop and reflect on my own leadership. More than just a "top 10 list," this book unlocks timeless principles of leadership that run deeper than the latest leadership fad."

Ted Esler, president, Missio Nexus

CONTENTS

To Bobby Clinton, my primary leadership mentor. Thank you for giving me "leadership eyes" to engage the Bible, and for modeling Bible-centered leadership.

The Reason and the Research Behind This Book

The Reason and the Research
Behind This Book

Executive Summary

The Bible is rich with leadership information. My research identified 1,090 leadership conversations in four major Leadership Eras of the Bible and documented the three basal elements of every interaction: the leader, the followers, and the situation. I then used a forced ranking process to identify the top ten leadership conversations in the Bible, which I examine in chapters one through ten. Beyond highlighting the findings of my research, my objective in this book is to stimulate your passion to engage the Bible as a primary source for leadership insight.

I am a lonely man, and yet I am not lonely. With my open Bible I live with prophets and priests, and kings; I walk and hold communion with apostles, saints, and martyrs, and with Jesus, and mine eyes see the King in His beauty and the land that is afar off....

My daily reading has brought me into company with the great prophets—Isaiah, Jeremiah, Ezekiel, Hosea, Micah, Malachi, and others—and I live again with them in the throbbing, tumultuous, teeming life of old Jerusalem, Samaria, Egypt, and Babylon. These prophets are old friends of mine.... They have blessed me a thousand times, kindled in me some of their flaming zeal for righteousness, their scorn of duplicity, pride, and worldliness, their jealousy for the living God; their fear for those who forget God and live as though He were not; their pity for the ignorant, the erring, the penitent; their anxiety for the future of their people; their courage in denouncing sin and calling men back to paths of righteousness.[1]

—Samuel Logan Brengle

Samuel Logan Brengle was born in rural Indiana in 1860. He grew up to become a shining star in the Salvation Army, with a powerful ministry as a speaker, writer, and godly leader, until his death in 1936. Brengle's faithfulness and consistent pursuit of God enabled him to maintain a vibrant faith right up to the end of his life. In his final days, he said:

I have sweet fellowship at times in my own room. The saints of all the ages congregate there. Moses is present, and gives his testimony, and declares that the eternal God is his refuge and underneath are the everlasting arms.

Joshua arises and declares, " ... as for me and my house, we will serve the Lord." Samuel and David, my dear friends Isaiah, Jeremiah, and Daniel, Paul and John and James, and deeply humbled and beloved Peter, each testify to the abounding grace of God.[2]

Brengle finished well.

I first encountered the life story of Samuel Logan Brengle while studying Leadership Emergence Theory at Fuller Theological Seminary with Dr. J. Robert Clinton, known as Bobby to his students. When I first read these words from Brengle, a deep hunger swelled up inside of me. I wanted to follow him as he followed Christ. I wanted to have this kind of personal, intimate, and transformational experience with God as revealed in the Bible. I wanted to finish well.

Two observations surfaced as I reflected on the desires stirred in my heart by Brengle's example.

First, there is no shortcut to this level of Bible engagement and spiritual intimacy. It requires discipline, consistency, and a spirit of openness to God over time. Brengle's words are rich, personal, and relational. He was not merely a Bible trivia expert. He described the leaders of Scripture as old friends who, through his daily reading, have blessed him a thousand times. He lived in the overflow of many years saturated by consistent time with God and fueled by the testimony and experiences of Bible characters.

You can't microwave a relationship. Imagine the foolishness of meeting someone for the first time and expecting to stay up talking all night and emerge the next day with a twenty-year friendship. That's not how relationships work.

It wasn't Brengle's knowledge of the Bible by itself that I found attractive. It was the depth of his intimacy with God and the role Bible characters played in stimulating that relationship over time.

Brengle's example challenged me to deeper and more consistent levels of Bible engagement for a lifetime. That's the only formula for the sweet fellowship he experienced in the closing days of his life. I want to know God like that and be surrounded in the here and now by the great cloud of witnesses who can inspire me to press on.

Second, a great way to learn leadership is from other leaders. And the Bible is full of leadership data. In military parlance, when it comes to leadership, the Bible is a target-rich environment. Brengle surrounded himself with the leaders of the Bible. He spent time with them daily, learned from them, and was transformed by their example. With his open Bible, he lived with prophets, priests, and kings, and he held communion with apostles and saints, and with Jesus.

Brengle said of his relationship with the apostle Paul:

> I am not sure that I lived so intimately with my darling ... wife as I have for many years lived with St. Paul. Far more constantly and intimately than he lived and travelled with his friend Barnabas and

his young Lieutenants, has he lived, travelled, slept, and talked with me.... I think Paul has been my greatest mentor, my most intimate spiritual guide.[3]

Brengle loved his wife. He said part of his mission in life was to make her happy.[4] He devoted himself to that mission in his lifelong marriage. Only against this backdrop can his words about Paul be fully understood.

How much time would I have to spend engaging the Scriptures to feel as though I had lived and traveled far more constantly and intimately with Paul than he did with his friend Barnabas and his young Lieutenants? What would it take to claim Paul as my greatest mentor and most intimate spiritual guide?

I'm not sure. But deep in my spirit a hunger awakened to find out.

Samuel Logan Brengle fully embraced the words of Hebrews 13:7, "Remember your leaders, who spoke the word of God to you. Consider the outcome of their way of life and imitate their faith."

Identifying Leaders in the Bible

In 2006, motivated in part by the Brengle-inspired desire to surround myself with leaders from the Bible, I began an ambitious personal study project with the goal of counting every leader from Genesis to Revelation. That project took about two years. It was tedious and time consuming, especially in the historical books, where the same narrative is covered in multiple books and requires careful cross-referencing to avoid double counting.

Early on, when I described my project to other leaders, several asked me, "How could you know if a person you are reading about in the Bible is actually a leader?" Their underlying assumption was clear: Giving someone a title or position doesn't make them a leader. Unless I could confirm the influence of biblical characters, I couldn't tell if they were leaders. And such information is not always available in the text.

Influence, not position, is at the core of leadership. When a person without leadership capacity is given a leadership title or position, the result isn't a complete lack of influence, but rather a greatly limited power base. This is true in life and in the Bible.

If you want to influence others, you will need some kind of power base—meaning a platform for influence. Non-leaders may have a leadership title or position, but they can't influence out of giftedness, competency, or consistent results. To influence followers, they have no choice but to leverage a negative power base by marshaling any available threat. In other words, their influence is almost never positive.

I decided to press forward with my leadership survey of the Bible. After two years of sifting through the Bible, verse by verse, I had my number. There are 1,181 leaders named in the Bible—1,073 in the Old Testament and 108 in the New Testament. Additionally, there are more than 13,000 other leaders referenced in the Bible but not named.

The Bible is rich with leadership data. I readily admit that my survey relied on an imprecise and subjective process. If I were to do it all over again, there is a good chance I'd come up with a slightly different number. But for me, it was only partly about the number. It was mostly about the opportunity to immerse myself, Brengle-style, in the lives of biblical leaders.

After the satisfaction of completing a project of this scope and magnitude wore off, I wasn't sure I had accomplished my greater goal. I now had Bible factoids borne out of primary research, but they weren't enough. Nonetheless, I needed a break from this kind of study project, so I set it aside.

Identifying Leadership Conversations in the Bible

By 2013 I was ready for another round of study. Leadership Emergence Theory teaches that the *basal elements* of every leadership interaction are the leader, the followers, and the situation. I began to consider a second pass through the Bible to identify all the leadership conversations and answer three questions about each one:

1. Who is the leader?
2. Who are the followers?
3. What is the situation?

The more I thought about it, the more convinced I became that this new study project would go deeper than simply counting leaders. It would give me a more powerful, more personal, more Brengle-like experience. It would also reinforce the discipline of my first project and cultivate the long-term habits needed to enlist Bible characters as my greatest mentors and most intimate spiritual guides.

For this second leadership survey of the Bible I soon realized the need for specific criteria to determine what leadership conversations to include or not include. I needed a way to answer the obvious question you're probably wondering about: How do you define a leadership conversation? Once again, this is a subjective process, but here's where I landed:

1. Conversations between people and God, or an angelic creature, would not be counted.

2. At least one of the people speaking had to be identified as a leader.

3. The specific words of at least one of the parties had to be identified as quotations in the text.

4. If the leader and the followers had some other relational connection, the conversation had to have a purpose beyond the relationship.

5. The interaction did not have to be face to face, but rather could be by messenger or letter, if the message was identified as a quotation and had a purpose beyond the relationship.

6. In conversations between two leaders of equal standing, the person exerting influence would be identified as the leader.

Unrecorded Words of Influence

Many places in the Bible imply but don't explicitly state a leadership conversation. I chose to limit the biblical leadership conversations included in my study to those where the words of the leader or follower are explicitly quoted in the text. But in doing so, some amazing leader-follower interactions had to be omitted. One of my favorites is implied in 1 Samuel 30:8–9.

The chapter begins with David returning to Ziklag with his raiding party, after being forced out of King Achish's army by Philistine soldiers. The soldiers had questioned David's loyalty as they prepared to do battle with Israel. When David and his men arrived at their base, they discovered the Amalekites had raided it, burned the tents, and taken captive the "women and all who were in it, both young and old."

David and his men "wept aloud until they had no strength left to weep." Devastated by the loss, David's men blamed him, and became "bitter in spirit," to the point they talked "of stoning him."

Showing the depth of his leadership instincts, "David found strength in the LORD his God," while his men wallowed in self-pity and blame. He then consulted with Abiathar the priest about whether to pursue the raiding party and if he would be successful. The word from God encouraged David to pursue the Amalekites. Verse eight ends with the assurance David would "succeed in the rescue." Then verse nine says: "David and the six hundred men with him came to the Besor Ravine." This is about as literal as "cut to the chase" can get. But the fast-forward in the story leaves out a leadership conversation I would have loved to hear. How did David convince his six hundred men not to stone him but to join him in pursuing the Amalekite raiding party?

We can assume he told them about the assurance he had received from God through Abiathar that their mission would be successful. David probably reminded them of other times he had heard a word from God about their raiding activity which had proved to be trustworthy (1 Sam. 23:1–6). I think this must have been one of the greatest locker room speeches any leader has ever given. But we'll have to discuss that with David in heaven someday, because the text is silent.

Considering Context in Four Eras of Biblical Leadership

When considering any situation in which a biblical leader interacts with followers, it is important to look beyond the immediate setting to the larger context. For example, the immediate setting of the situation could be:

- Dealing with a crisis (David with his men in 1 Sam. 30)
- Leading an army (Joshua in Ex. 17)
- Contesting unfair treatment (Jacob in Gen. 31)
- Resolving a conflict (the meeting in Acts 15)

The larger context helps explain the expectations followers have of leaders, which affects the way the immediate setting is perceived.

Modifying what I learned from Bobby Clinton[5], I explored this macro context by dividing the Bible into four Leadership Eras: Patriarchal, National, Transitional, and Spiritual.

The Patriarchal Leadership Era is characterized by family leadership, often with multigenerational families or clans. Abraham, Isaac and Jacob are the primary patriarchs of Israel, but this era stretches back to Job and includes other leaders in the book of Genesis.

The National Leadership Era includes pre-kingdom and kingdom components, from the time of the exodus through the time of the judges and into the establishment of Israel's monarchy. The pre-kingdom component ranges from a more centralized season under Moses to a less structured and decentralized time after Joshua, during the period of the judges.

The kingdom component includes the establishment of the monarchy, the dividing of Israel and Judah into two kingdoms, and the single expression of Judah after Israel's defeat and captivity by Assyria. Unlike the Patriarchal Era, the National Leadership Era is marked by kings, military and administrative political leaders, and by a fully developed prophetic ministry.

The Transitional Leadership Era stretches from the exile of Judah in Babylon through its return to Jerusalem. This era is characterized by strong leadership operating within or in subordination to pagan structures, both Babylonian and Persian. Transitional Leadership Era leaders such as Daniel, Ezra, and Nehemiah modeled deep spirituality and sparked renewal among both the exiles and the remnant that returned to rebuild the temple and the walls of Jerusalem. Prophetic leaders such as Haggai, Zechariah, and Malachi exhorted and inspired the people, encouraging faithfulness to God's ways.

The Spiritual Leadership Era encompasses pre-church and church components. The ministry of Jesus and the selection and development of the disciples dominate the pre-church component. The church component traces the expansion of the gospel beyond a Jewish context, characterized by new and loose structures that bypass the Jewish establishment. Spirituality is evidenced in all four Leadership Eras, but distinctly so in the ministry of Jesus and with the outpouring of the Holy Spirit. Leaders in this fourth era gain influence from their spirituality and from the development of spiritual gifts, more than from official titles in a formally recognized organizational chart.

Using the six criteria to identify leadership conversations, and dividing the Bible into four eras, I spent more than two additional years documenting leadership conversations, noting the leaders, the followers, and the situations in each case. By my count there are 1,090 leadership conversations in the Bible:

- 94 in the Patriarchal Era
- 701 in the National Era (261 pre-kingdom, 440 kingdom)
- 73 in the Transitional Era
- 222 in the Spiritual Era (160 pre-church, 62 church)

Digging Deeper for Leadership Insights, Principles, and Values

Unlike my first leadership survey of the Bible, my second pass to identify leadership conversations took me much deeper than trivia.

Repeatedly, I was lured into a sidebar study project, based on the intrigue flowing from how a leader interacted with followers in a specific situation. For example, I spent more than a month exploring the unique relationship Jeremiah had with the kings that ruled during his ministry.

As soon as I completed my documentation of leadership conversations, I knew I needed to review each of the four eras, looking for the most important leader-follower interactions in the Bible. A richer and more thorough analysis required another framework to answer another obvious question: How did you determine which conversations were most important?

I reviewed each of the four eras and identified the conversations that stood out as important. Then I filtered these conversations using four criteria framed by still more questions:

1. Scope and impact: What was the scope of this leadership conversation and how significant was the impact?

2. Counterfactual questions: What if this leadership conversation hadn't happened, or if the opposite had happened?

3. Law of emphasis: To what extent is this leadership conversation emphasized in the text, based on the number of verses devoted to it in the primary passage and references in other passages?

4. Redemption story: To what extent did this leadership conversation directly contribute to the grand narrative of redemption?

Scope and impact are generally straightforward to analyze. Counterfactual questions provide a "helpful hypothetical." We know nothing can thwart the ultimate purposes of God. But the sovereignty of God notwithstanding, counterfactual questions can help us identify the significance of a leadership conversation by engaging in a thought experiment that envisions what would or would not have happened if the response or outcome had been different.

The law of emphasis is a principle of biblical interpretation. It acknowledges that the Holy Spirit guided the authors of Scripture regarding what to include in the text and how much emphasis to give what they recorded. Some amazing leadership conversations implied or referenced in the Bible don't tell us anything about what was said, so they are not included in my study project.

When analyzing a leadership conversation, the law of emphasis gives us a way to measure importance based on the number of verses devoted to it, as a proxy for word count, and the number of times the interaction is referenced elsewhere in the Bible.

Finally, all the stories of the Bible fit together into the arc of a larger redemptive drama. But some people and experiences are more directly connected than others to God's plan to redeem humanity, which culminates in the ministry of Jesus as the Savior of the world and the birth of the Church.

After filtering my initial list of important leadership conversations from all four Leadership Eras, I force-ranked a list of the top ten. With those ten, I determined to go even deeper, looking for insights, principles, and values that could inform my own leadership.

Mining for Leadership Gold

Identifying a top ten list of leadership conversations in the Bible is like making plans to find the mother lode of a spiritual gold mine. To set up my drill rig for this mining project, I returned to the framework for analyzing leadership situations, using six lines of questioning that build off the basal elements of the leader, the followers, and the situation.[6] In the final chapter of this book, you will find a complete instruction manual to help you set up and operate your own spiritual mining project. You may also use these six lines of questioning to guide further study on any leadership interaction:

1. Who is the leader? What can we learn about his/her capacity in terms of talents, skills, and spiritual gifts? What can we learn about his/her sense of responsibility for leadership?

2. Who are the followers? What can we learn about followership in terms of: a) their loyalty to the leader; b) their acceptance of the leader's God-inspired vision; c) their willingness to serve and sacrifice to accomplish that vision; d) their responsiveness to correction or discipline; and e) the quality of relationships they have with each other and with the leader?

3. What is the leadership situation in terms of the Leadership Era? How does it affect the followers' expectations? What leadership functions—task, relationship, or inspiration—does the leader provide?

4. How does the leader attempt to gain influence with followers? Does the leader influence followers toward God's purposes?

5. What leadership insights, principles, and values can be observed? What are the results of the leader's actions? How would the followers have evaluated the leader's performance?

6. Are there any transferable principles to be gleaned from the leadership situation? How might leaders apply these principles today?

Asking these questions about any leadership interaction provides a practical way to analyze and extract meaningful information. These questions are especially helpful to engaging leadership situations in the Bible as we look for insights, principles, and values evidenced in the interaction of leaders and followers. I have visually referenced this approach as the leadership triangle.

The Leadership Triangle

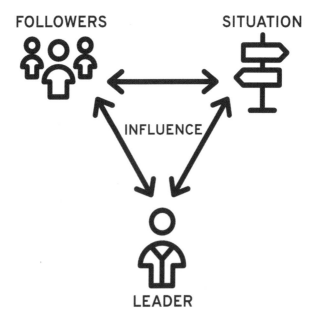

In chapters one through ten, I delve into my list of the ten most important leadership conversations in the Bible. I present them in order of occurrence, not importance, beginning with the Patriarchal Leadership Era and continuing through the National, Transitional, and Spiritual Leadership Eras. I have attached a specific theme to each leadership conversation, along with insights, principles, and values that can inform our leadership today.

Whether or not you agree with the criteria I used to identify and rank biblical leadership conversations, my objective in this book is to convince you of the wealth of leadership information in the Bible and to inspire your own journey of discovery.

Equipping Others to Explore Leadership Conversations in the Bible

Every meaningful conversation I've had about my leadership survey of the Bible has led to the same question: How and when are you going to share what you have learned? I didn't begin with a grand scheme, so my early response was: I don't know. But the genuine and universal interest piqued my curiosity enough to begin exploring the best approach.

But what does it look like to be a good steward of this research? I became convinced the best way forward would be to make my findings available to the widest possible audience on an open-source platform, free of charge. That's why I have now built a website—BibleCenteredLeadership.com—which provides access to a database of all the significant leadership conversations in the Bible. The database is searchable by:

- Leadership Era
- Book of the Bible
- Leader
- Topic

By providing access to the online database, I hope to inspire and equip an untold number of other personal study projects. I imagine leaders exploring all the leadership conversations in a specific Leadership Era or book of the Bible. Or leaders might study characters linked with topics, such as Moses and conflict, or Paul and mentoring, or David and vision.

This book is also a significant deliverable of my study project—and thank you for taking the time to read and perhaps also recommend it. Using the criteria and process I have already outlined, the book summarizes the high-level lessons gleaned from the top ten leadership conversations.

Reading and Studying with Leadership Eyes

The objective of this book is to stimulate your passion to engage the Bible as a primary source for leadership insight. I read more than twenty-five books every year. Almost all of them are about leadership, and only a few of them come from a Christian perspective. I'm not suggesting the Bible should replace your leadership learning from other sources. But the Bible should inform your leadership in a more intentional and systematic way than is common among Christian leaders today.

My mentor, Bobby Clinton, gave me a lifelong gift when he encouraged my development of "leadership eyes" for reading and studying the Bible. The training of most Christian leaders gives them theological and devotional lenses for the Bible. Clearly, our equipping would be inadequate without these. But as I've engaged leaders on the topic of leadership development, I've discovered very few who were taught how to engage the Bible as a primary source for leadership. I want to change that.

You might be pushing back a bit on my assertion. So let me engage you in a simple exercise I've done with hundreds of Christian leaders. I'm going to give you the first part of a Bible verse, and I want you to complete it. You may or may not be able to recall the chapter and verse number. But if you are interested enough in this topic to be reading this book, you are likely to be able to complete the verse. It has only ten words. I'll give you the first five:

"Jesus Christ is the same ..."
You fill in the rest.
Did you get it?
If not, go ahead and look it up. You can find it in Hebrews 13:8.

Now try another short verse.
This one has only nine words. I'll give you the first five:

"It is more blessed to ..."
You fill in the rest.
Likely you got this one as well. But if not, look it up in Acts 20:35.

What's the point of this exercise? You probably guessed, but let me state it outright: Both of these verses are about leadership, although they are rarely ever applied in that context.

Context is important for any student of biblical interpretation. Context is king, as we like to emphasize. But because it is so uncommon to think about the Bible as a source for leadership, we rarely consider leadership as part of the context. From the macro view of the Leadership Era to the micro view of each situation, we must consider it all.

In Hebrews 13:7–8, the verses fit together to establish a context. Verse seven, referenced at the beginning of this chapter, says: "Remember your leaders, who spoke the word of God to you. Consider the outcome of their way of life and imitate their faith." The leadership mandate[7] of this verse gives context to the following verse, which you completed above: "Jesus Christ is the same yesterday and today and forever."

As Bobby Clinton explains it, the whole point of verse eight—the unchanging nature of Jesus—is to reinforce a powerful message: The same divine force at work in the lives of leaders who have gone before us is available to you and me today. Because Jesus is unchanging, we are urged to consider the outcome of the way of life evidenced by great leaders of the Bible and the history of the church and to imitate their faith *in him*.

That's the lesson of the leadership mandate.

What about my second example? In Acts 20:35, Paul quoted Jesus when he said, "It is more blessed to give than to receive." We are not given the context in which Jesus spoke these words, as they are not referenced in any of the four Gospels. But we do have the context of when Paul quoted Jesus. Paul was wrapping up an invitation-only leadership meeting with beloved colleagues from Ephesus. He had labored with them for three years until he was forced to flee the city to escape a riotous crowd bent on killing him.

On his way to Jerusalem, Paul arranged to meet this select group of leaders in the coastal town of Miletus, in modern-day Turkey. In his closing words, Paul reminded these leaders how he had conducted himself among them. He had not coveted the possessions of others but rather had worked hard with his own hands to provide for himself and his companions. With this kind of hard work, Paul set an explicit example, which he reinforced with the words of Jesus: "It is more blessed to give than to receive."

In the context of this exclusive leadership gathering, we see Paul reminding his fellow leaders that he never used his position as a leader to take from others. He regarded leadership as a platform for serving others. Paul didn't want his colleagues to take advantage of the weak, nor use leadership to enrich themselves—something leaders in every culture and age are tempted to do.

As leaders today, our platform for influence is not about *getting*, it's about *giving*. Jesus set this example for us. The real blessing of leadership comes when we leverage our influence to benefit others, not ourselves.

The two examples in this simple exercise illustrate how easy it is to miss the leadership context of a biblical passage. And my leadership survey of the Bible convinced me you don't have to force the issue. The Bible is already rich with leadership data. We simply need to read and study it with leadership eyes.

In this book, and through the companion website, I want to go beyond presenting what I've learned from my leadership survey of the Bible. I want to help you, as a spiritual leader, catch a Brengle-like vision for intimacy with God, fueled and informed by the leaders of the Bible. I want to encourage you to live each day toward the goal of finishing well, surrounded and encouraged in your final days by the testimony of apostles, saints, and martyrs, all directing your attention to Jesus.

Let's get started.

CHAPTER 01

Favor

Favor

PATRIARCHAL
LEADERSHIP ERA

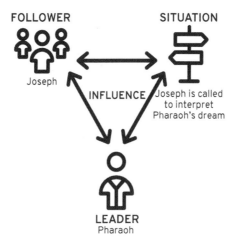

FOLLOWER   SITUATION

Joseph

INFLUENCE   Joseph is called
to interpret
Pharaoh's dream

LEADER
Pharaoh

So Pharaoh said to Joseph, "I hereby put you in charge of the whole
land of Egypt." —Genesis 41:41

Executive Summary

The favor principle asserts that giftedness and training are not
enough; to be effective as leaders we will need the favor of God. There
is a difference between the favor of God, and the power of God. The
power of God moves in or through *us* to impact *others* to advance
God's kingdom. The favor of God moves in or through *others* to
open doors for *us* to advance God's kingdom. Joseph's life shows
how God's favor took him from being sold into slavery to second in
command of Egypt.

Our video crew had no idea David would be on the flight that day—the last leg of a mission into a remote region of Asia. David, a native of the region, had chosen his name because it was easier for Westerners to pronounce. He spoke English and struck up a conversation with a member of the crew seated next to him on the plane.

Why did our crew want to visit this remote location?

It wasn't customary for tourists to venture into the rural villages where the crew planned to go. Our teammate explained that he was traveling with a group of Jesus-followers. The crew hoped to capture video footage that would enable us to tell the story of David's people and invite others to pray for God's blessing on their nation.

The idea intrigued David. He probed more deeply.

Where did the crew plan to go? What kind of footage did they hope to record?

The crew wanted simple scenes of people in everyday life that would tell their stories as authentically as possible. But David's people group, especially in this remote area, was not used to foreigners. They would not welcome outsiders into their villages, and certainly not into their homes. He was not at all optimistic about the prospects of the video project.

The only way to gain trust and access would be to have a local guide to advocate on the crew's behalf.

David had learned English from a Catholic priest and was very grateful for the kindness shown to him. He had always believed he would be able to repay that kindness to someone else.

Perhaps this was his chance.

Over the next few weeks David guided the crew through remote villages and religious sites that would never have been accessible otherwise. He became a crucial member of the crew.

Meanwhile, several other team members and I had traveled in a different direction. We went to an urban center in the region to do basic ethnographic research about the same people group. For several weeks, we conducted interviews and engaged in prayer walks surrounded by those we knew had very little opportunity to hear the gospel.

Our hearts were broken by the spiritual bondage we saw around us. It raised the sense of urgency we felt about the efforts of our video crew. We hoped they would capture compelling footage to help mobilize mission work among this people group.

The video and research crews reconnected at the airport on the way home. As the overall team leader, I was eager for a full report from the video crew. They described how David had helped them, and they were confident they'd gotten good video footage to reflect both the cultural heritage and spiritual need of David's people.

Later, when I first saw the footage, I thought I was watching a National Geographic documentary. The imagery provided the intimate perspective of an insider, as if the crew had loaned cameras to local families and asked them to record daily life in their homes, villages, and fields.

Ultimately, thousands of people saw the ten-minute video that told the story of David's people and motivated countless hours of prayer for the work of the gospel among them. The video played a catalytic role in launching a network of churches and organizations working to see Jesus proclaimed in that region and wherever clusters of this people group gathered.

Today, more than twenty years later, God is on the move among them.

God was already on the move on the flight that day when David struck up a conversation with our video crew. And when I think of what David did to help us, one word comes to mind: favor.

The Favor Principle

This is the favor principle: *Giftedness and training are not enough; to be effective as leaders we need the favor of God.*

Our video team was comprised of profoundly gifted business and ministry leaders. The primary videographer has gone on to found and lead a company that makes faith-friendly feature films shown in theaters all over the country. Another member of the team went on to author the definitive and comprehensive prayer guide on people groups in that region of the world. Yet another serves in a senior capacity with a widely recognized relief and development organization.

We had world-class people on our team, and they were well prepared. But they faced a set of circumstances where giftedness and training were not enough. They needed the favor of God. That favor was practically evidenced in David.

The idea of favor is all through the Bible. When the Israelites left Egypt, God made the Egyptians "favorably disposed toward the people, and they gave them whatever they asked for" (Ex 12:36). Ruth found favor with Boaz, first through his generosity in the fields and then as her kinsman redeemer. Ezra and Nehemiah found favor with kings who opened doors of opportunity and provided tangible support.

In Joseph's interaction with Pharaoh, one of the most important leadership conversations in the Bible, favor plays a major part in the backstory. But to appreciate how God showed favor *on* Joseph and *through* his leadership, consider the difference and the relationship between favor and power.

Favor and Power

The favor of God moves in or through *others* to open doors for *us* to advance his kingdom, whereas the power of God moves in or through *us* to impact *others* to advance his kingdom.

God's favor often comes through others who do not serve him and are not even aware of how or why they may be acting as his agents. "The king's heart is in the hand of the LORD; he directs it like a watercourse wherever he pleases" (Prov. 21:1).

God used Moses as an instrument of divine power released to compel the Egyptians to let the people of Israel go. But it was the favor of God moving on the Egyptians that allowed Israel to plunder their former captors on the way out. Giftedness and training were not enough; Moses and the people of Israel needed the favor of God.

Puff Graham

In 1949 Billy Graham hosted a series of evangelistic tent meetings in a Los Angeles parking lot. Organizers originally planned to host the meetings for three weeks but later extended the schedule multiple times. Ultimately Graham preached for eight weeks and attracted 350,000 people. As many as 3,000 professed faith in Jesus, including actors and radio personalities.

Several weeks in, the media mogul and publisher William Randolph Hearst sent a two-word directive by telegram to editors of his newspapers: "Puff Graham." In newspaper jargon, the directive told them to feature stories about Billy Graham and his event. Coverage about Billy Graham and his tent meetings received priority throughout Hearst's media empire. Soon other newspapers followed suit. Billy Graham and the gospel message gained momentum on a national stage.

When Billy Graham preached in Los Angeles, the power of God moved through him and drew people to Christ. When William Randolph Hearst sent a telegram to his editors, the favor of God moved through him.

Billy Graham wrote about this experience in his book, *Just As I Am*: "Hearst and I did not meet, talk by phone, or correspond as long as he lived."[8] Graham did not take credit, nor should we, for the way God's favor can open doors and accelerate results beyond anything we could do in our own strength.

Power without Favor

I had the privilege of attending Amsterdam 2000, a gathering of more than ten thousand evangelists from 190 countries, sponsored by the Billy Graham Evangelistic Association. Paul Finkenbinder, known throughout Latin America as Ermano Pablo, delivered one of the messages that impacted me most. He told a story from the early years of his ministry in Central America, where he was asked to translate for a visiting evangelist holding a series of rallies several nights in a row. God moved powerfully in those rallies, where many people came to saving faith and experienced healing.

One evening the evangelist invited people who wanted to be healed to come forward for prayer. So many people responded there simply wasn't room for the prayer counselors to engage each person individually. The evangelist instructed the people, wherever they were standing, to simply place their hands on the part of their body they wanted God to heal. Then he offered a prayer, which Paul translated.

Later that evening Paul reunited with his family and discovered that his young daughter, who had very poor eyesight and wore thick glasses, had placed her hands over her eyes during the healing prayer, and God had touched her. She no longer needed her thick glasses.

Paul couldn't wait to tell the news to the evangelist the next evening. He drove to the hotel earlier than the arranged time to pick up the speaker for the next rally. As he entered, he saw the man sitting at the bar, arm in arm with a prostitute. Unsure what to do, Paul went back to his car in the parking lot and waited.

When the time came for the pickup, he noticed the evangelist standing out in front of the hotel with his Bible tucked under his arm, ready to go. Paul spoke to the rally organizers about what he had seen at the hotel, and they intervened in the speaker's offstage behavior.

Paul learned an important lesson that night. Seeing many people respond to the evangelist's invitation to saving faith, and witnessing God's miraculous healing of his daughter, he came to understand: There is a difference between the power of God and the favor of God.

It is possible, at least for a season, to have the power of God moving through you, without the favor of God resting on you. God often chooses to honor the truth of his Word and the faith of the hearer, in spite of the messenger.

How Joseph Experienced the Favor of God

Except for the favor of God, little else could explain how Joseph went from being sold into slavery by his brothers to being "in charge of the whole land of Egypt" (Gen. 41:41). Pharaoh's request for Joseph's help to interpret his dreams is the culmination of Joseph's complicated journey in Egypt, marked every step of the way by the favor of God.

Joseph prospered under Potiphar in the house of his Egyptian master. The Lord gave Joseph success in everything he did, such that he "found favor" in Potiphar's eyes. Potiphar developed such deep trust that he placed his entire household under Joseph's care, and "did not concern himself with anything except the food he ate" (Gen. 39:6).

But Joseph ended up in prison after being accused of sexually assaulting Potiphar's wife, though he had resisted her advances. Even there, God was with Joseph, showing him kindness and "granting him favor in the eyes of the prison warden" (Gen. 41:21). Soon Joseph was "put in charge of all those in the prison, and responsible for all that was done there" (Gen. 41:22).

Years later, when Joseph interpreted Pharaoh's dreams and provided wise counsel, we see evidence of God's favor again, as Joseph was put "in charge of the whole land of Egypt" (Gen. 41:41).

Looking at Joseph's journey, and at many other examples of favor in the Bible, leaders might ask: Do I need the favor of God? A better question would be: How can I position myself for God's favor? And there's no simple answer. No favor formula can be applied like a math equation in a spreadsheet. But we can observe principles at work in Joseph's life story, which are worth emulating and can position us for God's favor to advance his redemptive purpose.

Positioning Yourself for Favor

We don't have to dig too deeply to discover the scope and impact of the leadership conversation between Joseph and Pharaoh. Joseph would later describe it to his brothers as "the saving of many lives." That claim was literally true, along with the spiritual implications flowing from the preservation of Israel, through whom the Messiah would come and fulfill God's promise through Abraham to bless all nations.

In Joseph's response to his experiences in Egypt, we find four attributes that help us understand what it looks like to position ourselves for the favor of God. Of these attributes, three can be cultivated in our leadership: purity, capacity, and humility. But the fourth, sovereignty, can only be found in God.

Purity

As defined in this chapter, favor is God moving in or through *others* to open doors for *us* to advance his kingdom. God's favor flows to all people, in that he worked through Jesus to extend saving grace as an expression of his great love for the world.

Nothing we can do, or not do, will change how much God loves us.

His love meter is stuck on unconditional. "God demonstrated his own love for us in this: While we were still sinners, Christ died for us" (Rom. 5:8). But the unmerited favor of God's saving grace does not extend to unmerited favor in every other area of life and leadership. You should not expect God to grant the favor needed to open doors of opportunity or expand your platform for influence if you engage in persistent disobedience. In as much as harboring sin disrupts our communication with God (Ps. 66:18), disobedience interrupts the flow of his favor. The story of Joseph's journey in Egypt reinforces the importance of purity, flowing from obedient choices. Joseph remains committed to purity despite repeated attempts by Potiphar's wife to seduce him. He "refused to go to bed with her or even be with her" (Gen. 39:10).

The intensity of temptation for leaders increases in direct proportion to their platform for influence. The higher you go in leadership, the greater the intensity of temptation—because you will not only be tempted to disobey, you will also be tempted to believe you have the power to cover up any indiscretions.

Joseph had a clear understanding of his platform for influence. He readily affirmed no one was greater in Potiphar's house than him. With him in charge, Potiphar did "not concern himself with anything in his house" (Gen. 39:8–9). Surely Joseph was tempted to believe he could cheat with Potiphar's wife and get away with it. But he recognized the invitation of Potiphar's wife as a "sin against God," from whom nothing can be hidden (Gen. 39:9).

Perhaps what took King David down was not just the temptation of a fling with Bathsheba. The power and influence of being king made him even more vulnerable, and he believed the lie that he could get away with it.

David's cover-up scheme started with inviting his soldier Uriah, Bathsheba's husband, to return from the front lines and give a report on the war. But Uriah refused to "eat and drink and lie with his wife" while his fellow soldiers slept in tents, away from the comforts of their homes. David, now drunk with power, had the audacity to send Uriah back to the front lines carrying what was essentially his own death warrant—a letter that instructed Joab to allow this honorable soldier to be killed in battle. Apparently, Uriah was so trustworthy that David knew he wouldn't make any attempt to read the letter he was carrying.

If Bathsheba discovered she was pregnant within six weeks of David sending for her, and she delivered their son at full term, Uriah would likely have been dead for at least six months before the prophet Nathan confronted David.

When David first held the son born of his adulterous relationship, he probably believed his elaborate scheme to cover up his sin had worked. But Nathan's rebuke provided two stark reminders: Nothing can be hidden from God, and persistent disobedience blocks the favor of God.

David never experienced the fullness of God's favor again. We know from the authentic testimony of Psalm 51 that David experienced the unmerited favor of God's forgiveness. But his personal life and leadership was marked by dysfunction and confusion for the rest of his life.

When as leaders we are tempted not only to disobey, but also to believe we can get away with it, we must remind ourselves that nothing can be hidden from God. When we fall, we must repent quickly and seek the unmerited favor of God's grace and forgiveness. Pray as David did, but sooner, "Create in me a pure heart, O God, and renew a steadfast spirit within me (Ps. 51:10). And position yourself for God's favor by committing, as Joseph did, to living a holy life.

Capacity

Giftedness in leadership or ministry capacity is not enough. We need God's favor to be effective. But those who fail to steward the gifts and talents God has given should not expect him to release favor as a means of compensating for chronic underachievement.

Joseph did not get to be in charge of Potiphar's household just because he was trustworthy. He rose to the highest position of authority because he was also effective. He developed his capacity and worked hard to produce results for Potiphar. The development of his capacity, along with a life of purity, did not go unnoticed by God.

In another biblical example of capacity, God gave Daniel and his three Hebrew friends "knowledge and understanding of all kinds of literature and learning" (Dan. 1:17). When tested by the king "in every matter of wisdom and understanding ... he found them ten times better than all the magicians and enchanters in his whole kingdom" (Dan. 1:20).

Daniel committed to a life of purity, refusing to defile himself with the royal food and wine. Over a period of three years, Daniel and the other exiles from Jerusalem received specific training to prepare them for service to the king (Dan. 1:5). God didn't give wisdom to Daniel and his friends to reward a lack of intellectual curiosity or a failure to apply themselves in the high-potential training program in which they found themselves in Babylon. Quite the opposite. They stood out because of their purity and capacity.

The favor of God sometimes results in an unexpected increase of a leader's platform for influence and corresponding visibility. When this happens, it is easy for onlookers to mistake favor for luck because the character-building choices that develop purity and capacity are often happening behind the scenes, out of the spotlight. Preparation may be separated by time from opportunity. Abraham Lincoln said, "I will prepare and someday my chance will come." One of my favorite historical mentors is A. T. Pierson. He became one of the most influential leaders of the late 1800s, especially in the world of missions, catapulted to prominence with the release of his book, *The Crisis of Missions*. Dana Robert, in her excellent biography on Pierson, described him as "the greatest promoter and most prolific writer about foreign missions in the late nineteenth century."[9]

The story of Pierson's rise to prominence illustrates how the development of a leader's capacity positions him for God's favor. Twenty years earlier, as a twenty-six year old pastor in upstate New York, Pierson found himself leading a church with a bigger vision for missions than his own. He came to believe "the interest and zeal of a congregation cannot ordinarily be expected to rise above the pastor's level."[10]

A. T. Pierson determined to grow his capacity as it related to missions so he could lead his church well. He began reading biographies of missionaries and explored the state of the world with a special focus on which countries were more open to the gospel message. He gathered statistical data and organized his thoughts to present lectures on individual mission fields, including stories of how the gospel was transforming lives, how cultures were being lifted with literacy programs, and how Christian ethics were taking root. Dana Robert explains Pierson's hard work:

> As he gathered all the facts and data he could find about modern missions, Pierson began collecting data that would one day result in hundreds of books and articles on the 'miracles of missions," the theory of missions, missionary biography, and the various types of missionary work.[11]

No one outside his small congregation in Waterford, New York, paid any attention to A. T. Pierson's diligent study and capacity-building discipline. But all that hard work did not go unnoticed by God.

In 1886, when Pierson was completing his book, the favor of God became evident in the form of a telegram from D. L. Moody, requesting help at a conference of 250 students from ninety colleges gathered for a month-long summer training program in Northfield, Massachusetts. Moody invited Pierson to speak to the students about the Bible and prophecy. But Robert Wilder, one of the students attending, knew about Pierson's upcoming book on missions and lobbied him to give a missionary challenge to the group. Since the teaching schedule was already in place, they arranged for an additional evening session.

One of the students in attendance, John R. Mott—later a key leader in the Student Volunteer Movement and a winner of the Nobel Peace Prize—described Pierson's address:

"On the evening of July 16, a special mass meeting was held at which Rev. A. T. Pierson gave a thrilling address on missions. He supported, by the most convincing arguments, the proposition that 'all should go and go to all.'"[12]

At Moody's Northfield conference, Pierson's years of quiet study and hard work that culminated in his book, *The Crisis of Missions*, intersected with the favor of God. It catapulted him forward in ways he never could have imagined as a twenty-something in an obscure community of upstate New York.

The opportunities that opened for Pierson because of the Northfield Conference and the publication of his book were the result of favor, not luck. But Pierson positioned himself for God's favor by years of discipline and hard work to build capacity while serving in relative obscurity.

Favor is never a shortcut. It is never a reward for mediocre service.

My friend and mentor, Cobie Langerak says, "Mediocrity is a bigger problem for Christian leaders than failure." Much of the half-hearted underachieving that gets passed off as "good enough for church work" would get you fired in the marketplace. Joseph cared deeply about the quality of his work for Potiphar. If you want the favor of God, and you will need it to be effective, seek purity and build capacity.

Humility

The more we develop capacity as leaders, the more tempted we are to take credit for results. Pride is the enemy of every believer. It is a special danger for every leader. Yet humility positions us for the favor of God because it reveals our dependency on him, and stimulates our faith in what only he can do. Andrew Murray said: "Faith and pride are enemies. Faith and humility are allies. We can never have more of genuine faith than we have of genuine humility."[13]

Later in this book, chapter eight is entirely focused on humility.

For now, Joseph and Daniel illustrate the way humility positions us to experience God's favor.

After Pharaoh summoned Joseph from prison to interpret a dream, Joseph responded with humility: "I cannot do it, but God will give Pharaoh the answer he desires" (Gen. 41:16). Remember, Joseph's track record for interpreting dreams created his window of opportunity to escape the unjust sentence in prison. But even while imprisoned, he affirmed to the cupbearer and baker that the interpretation of dreams belongs to God (Gen. 40:8).

Daniel offered a very similar response to King Nebuchadnezzar, when given the opportunity to interpret the king's dream, saying, "No wise man, enchanter, magician or diviner can explain to the king the mystery he has asked about, but there is a God in heaven who reveals mysteries" (Dan. 2:27).

Humility and its companions of dependency and faith often fly in the face of our leadership instincts. We tend to take charge and feel responsible to make something happen, rather than putting our faith in what God can do through us. Our pride seeks after and holds onto recognition from others. But as Andrew Murray said, "Pride makes faith impossible."[14] "And without faith, it is impossible to please God" (Heb. 11:6).

Humility rejects selfish ambition and undeserved praise. Jesus perfectly expressed the spirit of humility when he said, "The Son can do nothing by himself" (John 5:19).

We see the connection between great humility and great faith in two people Jesus singled out as examples. [15] In Matthew 8, a Roman centurion approached Jesus, asking for help on behalf of a paralyzed servant who was suffering greatly. Jesus offered to go and heal the servant. The centurion responded with great humility that he did not deserve to have Jesus come under his roof. However, the centurion was a man in command of other soldiers. He was accustomed to giving orders. Therefore he believed his servant would be healed if Jesus simply gave the order.

Matthew 8:10 tells us how Jesus acknowledged the centurion's humility: "When Jesus heard this, he was astonished and said to those following him, 'I tell you the truth, I have not found anyone in Israel with such great faith.'"

On another occasion, recorded in Matthew 15, a Canaanite woman approached Jesus to plead on behalf of her daughter, who was suffering from a demonic attack. Jesus ignored the woman, and the disciples tried to send her away. But she persisted with great humility: "Even the dogs eat the crumbs that fall from their master's table" (Matt. 15:27). Jesus responded to her, "Woman, you have great faith! Your request is granted" (v. 28).

Let these examples inspire us as leaders to humble ourselves in dependency and faith.

Sovereignty

Purity, capacity, and humility position us for God's favor. But the combination of these attributes does not create a spiritual spreadsheet formula that automatically adds up to God's favor. Because there's a fourth attribute needed: God's sovereignty.

Joseph's story illustrates how God's sovereignty overlaps with purity, capacity, and humility. After being falsely accused by Potiphar's wife, Joseph was placed in prison. While he was there, he interpreted the dreams of the baker and cupbearer, and he pleaded with the cupbearer to "remember him and show him kindness" (Gen. 40:14). "The chief cupbearer, however, did not remember Joseph; he forgot him" (Gen. 40:23). And it took two years before the cupbearer's memory was jogged by Pharaoh's dreams.

Why the delay? Was it that Joseph did not yet qualify for the favor of God? We know that is not true because the text says:

> But while Joseph was there in the prison, the LORD was with him; he showed him kindness and granted him favor in the eyes of the prison warden. So the warden put Joseph in charge...the warden paid no attention to anything under Joseph's care, because the Lord was with Joseph and gave him success in whatever he did. (Gen. 39:20-23)

Joseph experienced God's favor in prison while he waited for more favor to come on God's sovereign timeline.

Petitioning God for Favor

Favor is valuable for everyone. It is essential for leaders. Our giftedness and training are not enough; to be effective in ministry and leadership we need the favor of God. Many open doors will hinge on favor more than giftedness. When we need favor the most, there is nothing we can do in the moment to get it.

Leaders in every sector need favor, but the need is more critical for nonprofit and ministry leaders who regularly face the challenge of raising funds and mobilizing volunteers. Every day, their meetings and interactions depend on the favor of God. Therefore, the prayer life of every Christian leader should include a regular focus on petitioning God for favor.

When Nehemiah cried out to God in preparation for his meeting with King Artaxerxes, he said, "Give your servant success today by granting him favor in the presence of this man" (Nehemiah 1:11). When Esther, who will be the focus of chapter seven, was encouraged by Mordecai to approach King Xerxes to advocate for her people, she not only spent three days in prayer and fasting, she asked Mordecai to invite all the Jews in Susa to fast and pray with her. She clearly recognized the need for favor.

To position ourselves for God's favor we must walk in purity, develop our capacity, and live a life of humility. We must also acknowledge God's sovereignty as we boldly ask him to give us favor.

CHAPTER 02

Perspective

Perspective

NATIONAL
LEADERSHIP ERA

FOLLOWERS   **SITUATION**

People
of Israel   INFLUENCE   Twelve spies
are sent by
Moses to explore
the land of
Canaan and bring
back their report

LEADER
Twelve Spies

"We seemed like grasshoppers in our own eyes, and we looked the same to them." —Numbers 13:33

Executive Summary

Perspective is a leadership differentiator. Leaders see what followers don't. The most effective leaders see what other leaders don't. Perspective is to life what a scale is to a map. It helps us see clearly where we are, in relation to where we've been, and where we want to go. As leaders, we grow in effectiveness as we learn to interpret life more and more from God's vantage point. The leadership conversation between Moses and the twelve spies helps us understand the need for better perspective on ourselves, our situation, our strategy, and our success.

My oldest daughter decided to try out for the cheerleading squad when she was in high school. I was surprised. She had never shown much of an interest in sports, but she is extroverted. After making the squad she was excited about the idea of sharing the experience with friends.

The first football game of the season was away, so I dropped my daughter off at the school and returned later that afternoon to pick her up. On the drive home, I struck up a conversation that went something like this:

"So, how'd the team do?"
"Pretty good."
"What was the score?"
"Thirty-six to nothing."

Since my daughter didn't have a deep knowledge of sports, and since I'm a total sports fanatic, I felt a fatherly responsibility to coach her.

"Wow, that's more than *pretty good*. That's *really good*. Either your team is awesome or the team you played stinks, but in any case, that's a great start to the season."

After looking at me like I was clueless, my daughter decided to set me straight.

"Oh, we didn't win."

Now I really felt like I had some coaching to do.

"OK, if the score was thirty-six to nothing, and your team didn't win, I'm sure the coach wouldn't describe the team's performance as *pretty good*. We can only hope the team will get better over the course of the season."

With a look of disappointment on her face, my daughter decided it was time to coach me.

"Dad, some of the other cheerleaders said when we played this team last year, we didn't even get to do the first-down cheer. This year, we got to do the first-down cheer. Twice. We did *pretty good*."

The sports fan in me wanted to remind her that you don't get points for first downs. But I was wise enough to let her have the last word. And one simple phrase echoed through my mind: It's all about perspective.

To quote Bobby Clinton, "The difference between leaders and followers is perspective. The difference between leaders and effective leaders is better perspective."

Perspective is to life what a scale is to a map. It helps us see clearly where we are in relation to where we've been and where we want to go. As Jesus-following leaders, we gain better perspective as we increasingly see and understand the circumstances of life from God's vantage point. Jesus spoke to the importance of perspective when he said: "Your eye is the lamp of your body. When your eyes are good, your whole body also is full of light. But when they are bad, your body also is full of darkness" (Luke 11:34). But for leaders, perspective is more than important. It's crucial.

The Power of Perspective in Leadership

The story of the twelve spies sent by Moses to explore the land of Canaan is a case study in the power of perspective in leadership. At the Lord's command, Moses identified one leader from each of the ancestral tribes to scout out the promised land of Canaan.

By this time in the National Leadership Era, a complex leadership structure had begun to evolve among the Israelites. A variety of terms used in the text identify different roles in this emerging structure. I'll use terms such as elder, official, or judge, based on what is in the text.

Jethro consulted with Moses, instructing him to appoint officials over thousands, hundreds, fifties, and tens. The officials served as judges to settle disputes among the people (Ex. 18:21). Each tribe had a leader, appointed from the community (Num. 1:19).

God set apart a group of seventy elders by taking the Spirit that was on Moses, putting it on them, and causing them to prophesy (Num. 11:25). Another group of more than 250 well-known community leaders had been appointed to a council[16] (Num. 16:2).

Given the complex layers of leadership among the Israelites, it was no small assignment to be selected by Moses to spy out the land of Canaan. This group of twelve leaders represented the first formal team assigned a specific task on behalf of the entire nation in the National Leadership Era. It is easy to read the familiar verses of this story without considering the significance of how it must have felt to be publicly identified for this responsibility.

The instructions were clear. Moses wanted a report on the land. Is it good or bad? Is the soil fertile or poor? Are there trees or not? He also wanted a report on the people. Are they strong or weak? Few or many? Are their towns unwalled or fortified? Moses added one more request, asking the spies to do their best to bring back some fruit as visual evidence of the land's promise (Num. 13:17–20).

In the text, the instructions from Moses do not include a timeline. The exploration took forty days; we don't know for sure if this was intentional or coincidental. But it was plenty of time for anticipation and expectation to build among the Israelites. God had promised not only to deliver them from bondage but also to bring them to the land that had been sworn "with uplifted hand ... to Abraham, to Isaac, and to Jacob." Through Moses, God had once again made his promise to Israel about this land, "I will give it to you as a possession. I am the LORD" (Ex. 6:8).

Now, twelve representative leaders were carrying out their assignment as spies, and in a matter of weeks they would bring a full report. Their mission must have been the topic of conversation among the Israelites at every meal, every campfire.

We don't have any information about the team dynamics of the twelve spies while they were exploring the land. The text is also silent regarding the conversations they must have had to prepare the official report for Moses and the people. We know there was disagreement, maybe at times heated. Caleb and Joshua, two of the most well-known spies, were likely in favor of taking the land. Perhaps some were undecided, and still others were convinced that any attempt to invade would be suicidal.

The initial report appears to be fact-based and backed by all twelve spies. The land flowed with milk and honey, just as God had said. A single cluster of grapes, along with pomegranates and figs, provided proof of fertile land.

The spies also reported that the people of Canaan were powerful and lived in large, fortified cities. The Canaanites included descendants of Anak, the Amalekites, Hittites, Jebusites, Amorites, and Canaanites. Neither Joshua nor Caleb ever disputed these facts.

Better perspective is always grounded in reality. It does not ignore obstacles or challenges. Perspective is not the same as positivity. Leaders with better perspective are more likely to be positive. But you can be positive without better perspective. Frankly, that's what my daughter was doing when she affirmed, on the losing end of a thirty-six-to-zero score, that the football team had done pretty good.

Joshua and Caleb were not pretending. They believed everything God had promised. That's how they gained better perspective, seeing the challenge before them through God's eyes.

Same Data, Different Perspective

Caleb didn't speak until the initial data about the land had been reported. And he made no attempt to contradict what had been said. He simply affirmed they should "go up and take possession of the land," for they could certainly do it (Num. 13:30). The other leaders, Joshua excluded, "spread among the Israelites a bad report about the land they had explored" (Num. 13:32).

The climactic statement in the bad report is one of the most interesting mash-ups of hyperbole and metaphor imaginable: "We seemed like grasshoppers in our own eyes, and we looked the same to them" (Num. 13:33). Remember, the spies were selected because they were already influential leaders. We should not be surprised that the people followed the majority report. But the majority report was so bad it could be reduced to the status of insects. Whatever excitement and expectancy had been building during the forty-day wait had withered to disappointment and resentment. "That night all the people of the community raised their voices and wept aloud" (Num. 14:1).

By this time, the Israelites had become a nation of at least one million people, with more than six hundred thousand adult men who were able to serve in its army (Num. 2:45–46). It would have been impossible for Moses to converse with so many people at the same time. Within the nation's complex leadership structures, a recognized group of leaders would have represented the people before Moses.

As the bad report spread throughout the camp, the people's furor came to a head. The leaders of the community came to Moses with a ridiculous assertion:

> If only we had died in Egypt! Or in the desert! Why is the LORD bringing us to this land only to let us fall by the sword? Our wives and children will be taken as plunder. Wouldn't it be better for us to go back to Egypt (Num. 14:2–3)?

In response to their foolish questions, Moses and his brother Aaron fell to the ground, perhaps partly from the emotional shock and partly as a sign of throwing themselves at the mercy of God. Joshua and Caleb could not keep silent. They leveraged their status as part of the original group of spies to present a better perspective:

> The land we passed through and explored is exceedingly good. If the LORD is pleased with us, he will lead us into that land, a land flowing with milk and honey, and will give it to us. Only do not rebel against the LORD. And do not be afraid of the

people of the land, because we will swallow them up. Their protection is gone, but the LORD is with us. Do not be afraid of them (Num. 14:7–9).

Everyone was operating from the same data. The land was good. The people were powerful. But there were different perspectives. The situation among the Israelites reflects human nature without the influence of effective leadership. Everyone prefers the *results* of positive change to the stagnation of the status quo. Yet many people prefer the status quo to the *effort* required to produce positive change. The difference between the two preferences is almost always a matter of perspective.

Better Perspective for Leading Well

Perspective is a leadership differentiator. Leaders see what followers don't. The most effective leaders see what other leaders don't. Like Joshua and Caleb, we need better perspective. We grow in leadership effectiveness the more we learn to interpret life from God's vantage point, which gives us a better perspective. We can gain better perspective on ourselves, our situation, our strategy, and our success.

Better Perspective on Ourselves

Self-awareness is the primary gateway into effective self-leadership. Each of us must understand ourselves well to lead ourselves well. A simple definition of self-awareness includes two facets: first, being honest with yourself about yourself and second, being honest about yourself with others.[17]

As Jesus-following leaders, we can be tempted to view self-awareness as an attempt to marry psychology and self-help with spiritual leadership. Not so. Every person's journey of faith begins with an epiphany of self-awareness directed by the Holy Spirit. It starts with being honest with yourself about yourself—by admitting you are a sinner and incapable of changing on your own. Next comes being honest about yourself with others, especially God—by affirming how much you need Jesus as Savior.

Spiritual self-awareness begins with salvation but doesn't end there. As self-aware leaders, we gain better perspective because we understand our strengths and gaps. We know who God made us to be, and how to leverage our strengths, in the power of the Holy Spirit, to do the good works God prepared in advance for us to do (Eph. 2:10).

As we become highly self-aware, we discover new levels of confidence and clarity about how God has equipped us to add value to other individuals and contribute to a team. We come to understand where we should give priority to growth and how we are vulnerable to derailing our own leadership.[18]

The ten spies who spread a bad report among the Israelites did not have good perspective on themselves. Otherwise they never would have viewed themselves as grasshoppers. Better leadership perspective requires seeing ourselves more and more in line with how God sees us.

Grasshopper Moments

The admission of the ten spies that they "seemed like grasshoppers" in their own eyes is a classic example of the need for better perspective. As a leader, I confess to having my own "grasshopper moments."

In the spring of 2006 I accepted an invitation by the board of directors for the Evangelical Fellowship of Mission Agencies (EFMA) to serve as its president and CEO.[19] One of my first responsibilities as president was to represent the EFMA at a week-long World Evangelical Alliance Mission Commission consultation in South Africa, where I would have the opportunity to introduce myself to many mission leaders.

I had come into my role with EFMA as an outsider. I had never served with one of its member organizations, nor attended any event it had sponsored. I was the classic unfiltered leader.[20]

Every networking conversation that week went pretty much the same way. Whenever I met someone, they'd ask what I had been doing before taking on my new role. I'd explain how I had worked for more than a decade in the field of young leader training. Then they'd look confused. It seemed nearly impossible for anyone to figure out how I'd gotten from there to here. One mission agency CEO actually asked me over lunch, "Do you have any idea what the board was thinking when they hired you?"

That was my grasshopper moment.

I wanted to go back to my hotel room and hide under the bed for the rest of the week. I called my wife and told her that accepting this role may have been the biggest mistake of my life. I couldn't wait for the week to end. And I tried to be as invisible as possible, slipping into meetings a little late, and skipping some meals altogether.

On the last full day of the event, I slithered into the room that had Wi-Fi so I could check my email. I sat off to the side with my head down, minding my own business. But one of the other leaders in the room approached me, saying he had seen me throughout the week but hadn't yet had a chance to introduce himself. He was Greg Livingstone, founder of the mission agency, Frontiers. I knew exactly who he was. I told him my name but not my role, hoping I wouldn't fall down the rabbit hole I'd been avoiding for days. But Greg probed more specifically, so I told him I was the newly appointed leader at EFMA.

Greg's eyes bugged out, and his countenance brightened. "So you're the new guy! I've been hoping to meet you. Can you have dinner with me tonight?"

Over dinner Greg asked me about my week. Believing I had little to lose, I was transparent with him about my grasshopper moment. Without revealing who said what, I explained to Greg that many mission CEOs were struggling to understand how I got appointed to lead the EFMA. And for the next hour Greg Livingstone radically changed my perspective. He asked questions about my journey and described why he believed my experiences had uniquely prepared me for this opportunity. I'll never forget the passion in his voice when he said, "I think appointing you at this moment may have been the best decision the EFMA board has made in twenty-five years."

Greg's words about my appointment may sound as hyperbolic as the ten spies who thought they were grasshoppers. But God used him to help me gain better perspective on myself. It was a God moment I'll never forget.

In the book of Judges, Gideon experiences a grasshopper moment too. An angel of the LORD approached him with a challenge to lead his people in battle against the Midianites. This story presents a classic contrast of perspectives.

Listen to Gideon's perspective on himself: "How can I save Israel? My clan is the weakest in Manasseh, and I am the least in my family" (Judg. 6:15).

His words expose an important lesson. We can lose perspective when we compare ourselves with others. Gideon compared his clan to other clans, and himself to others in his family. Every leader understands this temptation. We compare who we are, and the role God has given us, with other leaders.

Sometimes we compare ourselves with people we believe have less capacity and status, because we want to feel more important. Other times we fall into the trap of comparing ourselves with leaders who have bigger platforms for influence, and we end up feeding our insecurities. Comparison is a road with deep ditches on both sides. The Devil doesn't really care which ditch you fall into.

In contrast, the angel of the LORD affirms God's perspective on Gideon, saying, "The LORD is with you, mighty warrior" (Judg. 6:12). The term *mighty warrior* could literally be translated *mighty force*. The Hebrew meaning can indicate a person as a mighty force because of great wealth, a strong army, or depth of character. If the first part of Judges 6:12 is true—"The LORD is with you"—then the last part of the verse is also true—"you are a mighty force"— regardless of whether you need resources, protection, or the strength of character to do what is right.

The validation of your leadership, like Gideon's, has nothing to do with how you compare to others. It has everything to do with a better perspective on yourself, especially this assurance: The Lord is with you as you pursue what he has called you to do. Joshua and Caleb found confidence to take the promised land because they believed, "the LORD is with us" (Num. 14:9).

Better Perspective on Our Situation

Max DePree said the first responsibility of leaders is to define reality. The basal elements of every leadership interaction are the leader, the followers, and the situation. Leaders are called upon to influence followers toward God's purposes for followers in a specific situation. We become more effective leaders as we develop better perspective on our situation.

Joshua and Caleb never challenged the facts of the situation described by the other ten spies. These two leaders brought a very different perspective to the situation while their fellow spies admitted they seemed like grasshoppers in their own eyes and assumed they looked the same to the Canaanites.

I have often wondered how the spies could possibly have known what the people of Canaan thought about them. I don't have any experience with espionage, but I doubt they went around doing interviews saying, "Hey we're making plans to take over this land and before we do, we'd like to ask, what do you think about us?"

Our leadership perspective becomes distorted not only by what we think of our situation, it is also distorted by what we think other people think of our situation. When our thinking is based on faulty perspective, what we believe others think is also tainted. Leaders with a flawed perspective on themselves are especially vulnerable to projecting that perspective onto their situation.

Joshua and Caleb emphasized a better perspective in their final plea to the leaders of Israel: "Do not be afraid of the people of the land, because we will swallow them up" (Num. 14:9). This perspective on the situation was correct and would be confirmed forty years later by the testimony of two other spies.

After Joshua succeeded Moses as the leader of Israel, the Israelites began to prepare for another opportunity to enter the land of Canaan. Joshua secretly sent two spies to explore. Perhaps he had learned a lesson from Moses and therefore sent a smaller group without public fanfare to minimize the possible impact of a negative report. Rahab hid the two spies and protected them from the king of Jericho.

Before the spies retired for the night on Rahab's rooftop, she gave them an amazing report:

> I know that the LORD has given this land to you and that a great fear of you has fallen on us, so that all who live in this country are melting in fear because of you. We have heard how the LORD dried up the water of the Red Sea for you when you came out of Egypt.... When we heard of it, our hearts melted and everyone's courage failed because of you, for the LORD your God is God in heaven above and on the earth below (Josh. 2:8–11).

Let this sink in for a moment. Rahab explained how the miracles God performed *before the first group of spies explored the land*, including parting the Red Sea, had already caused the Canaanites' hearts to melt and their courage to fail. Forty years later, the people of Canaan still remembered the miracles God had done on behalf of Israel, and were convinced that the LORD "is God in heaven above and on earth below."

The minority opinion of Joshua and Caleb had been right all along.

Don't Wait for Hindsight

We understand the wisdom that hindsight is twenty-twenty. Some day we will be able to look back on the happenings of life and make sense of even the most confusing circumstances. The generation that survived wandering in the desert and entered the land with Joshua and Caleb could look back on forty years unnecessarily wasted.

But you don't have to wait for the benefit of hindsight. That's not leadership.

Sometimes the situation in which we find ourselves is difficult, without exaggeration. We live and lead in a fallen world, marked by sin, tragedy, and disease. When disaster strikes in the form of a health crisis, financial pressure, or a thousand other forms of pain, we are all drawn to ask, *Why is this happening?* Wise leaders seek a better perspective by asking a better question, *Who is in control?* When we gain better perspective on our situation we can more quickly recognize life-shaping experiences and respond properly to them. God uses everything in life to prepare us for everything in life. Every experience can be used to shape our character and accelerate our development.[21] But the reverse is also true. When we fail to recognize how God is at work and therefore fail to respond properly, our lack of perspective slows our progress.

Shifting our focus from *why* to *who* prevents us from falling into a sinkhole of bitterness and blame. God is in control. God is good. We can affirm—even in the midst of the challenges and without the benefit of hindsight—that God can redeem anything for good.

Better Perspective on Our Strategy

Hope is not a strategy. But leaders without hope almost never develop a good strategy. When we lose perspective on ourselves, we also lose perspective on our situation. When we don't have perspective on our situation, it becomes nearly impossible to develop a winning strategy.

After hearing the situation summed up by the twelve spies, Caleb put forward a strategy informed by God's promise: "We should go up and take possession of the land, for we can certainly do it" (Num. 13:30). But the bad report of the ten spies swept through the leadership layers of Israel like an epidemic. They succumbed to hopelessness.

And, as often happens, hopelessness then gave way to foolishness. This emotional cancer is especially perilous when it happens to leaders because they have influence over followers. The top leaders of Israel[22]—except for Moses, Aaron, Joshua, and Caleb—countered with the following foolish strategy: "We should choose a leader and go back to Egypt" (Num. 14:4).

Joshua and Caleb then responded by making one final appeal to the leaders of Israel, with a reminder that the land was "exceedingly good" (Num. 14:7). Failing to take the land would be rebelling against the LORD. They exhorted the people not to be afraid, because the protection of the Canaanites "was gone" and God was with Israel. But the people were unmoved. They even talked of stoning Joshua and Caleb, along with Moses and Aaron.

Perspective or Presumption?

At this point in the story, God intervened. "The glory of the LORD appeared at the Tent of Meeting to all the Israelites" (Num. 14:10). Moses had an extraordinary encounter with God at the tent of meeting as he interceded for the very people who had talked of stoning him. Moses emerged from his encounter with God ready to report God's response to the contemptuous behavior of the Israelites. The news was grim: The ten spies would be put to death by God, the people would wander in the desert for forty years—one year for every day the spies explored the land—and everyone age twenty or older would die in the desert.

When Moses reported that the ten spies had been struck down and had died of a plague before the LORD, the people mourned bitterly. The next day they came back to Moses with a new strategy: "We will go up to the place the LORD promised" (Num. 14:40). But Moses responded by asking:

> Why are you disobeying the LORD'S command? This will not succeed! Do not go up, because the LORD is not with you. You will be defeated by your enemies ... because you have turned away from the LORD, he will not be with you and you will fall by the sword (Num. 14:41–43).

Twenty-four hours earlier, taking the land was a winning strategy, and refusing to do so was rebelling against God. Now, going up to the land would be disobeying God and doomed to failure.

But never mind the warning of Moses. The Israelites "in their presumption" went into battle without Moses and without the ark of the covenant moving from the camp (Num. 14:44). They were immediately defeated.

We see here the difference between presumption and perspective. It is a dangerous thing for leaders to put forward a strategy and presume God is on board. Sadly, it happens all the time.

Perhaps we would all be better off if presumptuous plans were exposed immediately by failure. But they are not. In Numbers fourteen, the sin of presumption resulted in literal death. Today it produces lifeless, manufactured results, regardless of how much we hype them.

A. W. Tozer once spoke about presumptuous leadership in the church, saying that if the Holy Spirit were removed, the church would keep moving forward without anyone noticing a change. Paul described presumption as building with wood, hay, or straw. He warned that "the fire will test the quality of each person's work" (1 Cor. 3:13).

The universal lesson embedded in this conversation is simple, yet powerful. Discernment is more important than strategy, and obedience is the highest form of execution. Sometimes God asks leaders to embrace a strategy that can only be understood through the lens of obedience, like asking Gideon to pare down his army to three hundred men or telling Joshua to march around Jericho instead of attacking it.

My personality profile predisposes me to think big picture. *Strategic* is the top result in my StrengthsFinder assessment. I've read many books on strategy and worked hard at refining models that help organizational leaders develop a strategic plan. But better perspective on strategy hinges on our ability as leaders to discern the course of action that will be permeated by the presence of God.

In discernment, our conversation with God through prayer is crucial. Moses modeled leadership that pursues intimacy with God and a prayer life that supported the strategic action steps God directed. Seeing this prayer life in action helps us understand how Joshua gained better perspective on success.

Better Perspective on Our Success

The story of the twelve spies doesn't end with success. But forty years later, Joshua led confidently and obediently to take the land of Canaan—perhaps because he had already learned the importance of gaining better perspective on success.

We first meet Joshua on the pages of Scripture when Moses instructed and reassured him: "Choose some of our men and go out to fight the Amalekites. Tomorrow I will stand on top of the hill with the staff of God in my hands" (Ex. 17:8–9).

Aaron and Hur were with Moses on the top of the hill while Joshua was leading his chosen men into battle. Moses lifted his hands in prayer for the army during the battle. From time to time, Moses rested his arms by lowering them to his side. At some point in the battle, Moses made a connection that when his arms were up, "the Israelites were winning," and when he lowered them, "the Amalekites were winning" (Ex. 17:11).

This very familiar story reminds leaders of the power and priority of prayer. But I don't believe God intended this experience primarily for Moses. I believe God set up this unusual experience, that so far as we know was never repeated, to give Joshua better perspective on his success.

After the battle was over and "Joshua overcame the Amalekite army with the sword," God told Moses to make a written record of the battle "as something to be remembered and *make sure Joshua hears it*" (Ex. 17:14, emphasis mine).

It had to be exciting for Joshua to emerge victorious from his first experience as a battlefield commander. We have no reason to believe he did other than but fight bravely and employ good military strategy. In this moment of success God wanted Joshua and us to learn an extraordinary object lesson, so he directed Moses to share it. We can imagine Moses explaining: *Joshua, you did not win because of your bravery or your strategy. Those surges from the Amalekite army happened exactly when my arms were lowered. Your army prevailed when my arms were raised. God wants you to understand a very important lesson from your very first battle: Victory comes from God. You need this perspective on your success. Don't ever forget it.*

Better Perspective for Finishing Well

Of the 1,181 leaders identified by name in the Bible, we have enough information in the text to study the lives of about one hundred of them. From those one hundred, only one in three finished well.[23] This fraction should be a reality check for us as leaders. The odds are not in our favor.

One of the keys to finishing well is to view our present leadership with a lifetime perspective.[24] To say Joseph took the long view would be an understatement. He was so convinced God would eventually give the Israelites the promised land that he "made the sons of Israel swear an oath, and said, 'God will surely come to your aid, and then you must carry my bones up from this place'" (Gen. 50:25). When Moses led the Israelites out of Egypt, he "took the bones of Joseph with him, because Joseph had made the sons of Israel swear an oath" (Ex. 13:19).

Joshua, a close aide to Moses and eventually his successor, would inherit responsibility for this task. And when the Israelites had finally conquered the land of Canaan, Joshua made good on the oath by burying Joseph's bones at Shechem, in the tract of land Jacob had purchased from the sons of Hamor (Josh. 24:32).

We don't know for sure who had responsibility for Joseph's bones at the crucial moment when the spies first explored the land. But Joshua, as a confidant of Moses, clearly knew why they carried Joseph's bones out of Egypt. And maybe Joshua borrowed some faith from Joseph, regarding God's promise to give the Israelites the land. And maybe that faith helped him maintain a better perspective on himself, his situation, his strategy, and his eventual success.

CHAPTER 03

Change

Change

NATIONAL
LEADERSHIP ERA

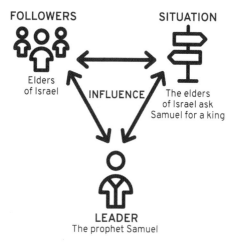

FOLLOWERS   SITUATION

Elders
of Israel   The elders
                             of Israel ask
INFLUENCE   Samuel for a king

LEADER
The prophet Samuel

"You are old, and your sons do not walk in your ways; now appoint a king to lead us, such as all the other nations have." —1 Samuel 8:5

Executive Summary

Leadership is complex, problematic, and filled with risk, which is why good leaders are needed. Complexity is amplified in situations that involve major change. A primary change management skill is the ability to anticipate the unintended consequences of change. Israel's request for a king triggers one of the most complex change journeys in the Bible. The Israelites did not merely reject Samuel's sons as their leaders; they asked for a totally new leadership structure. The transition from theocracy to monarchy expanded the power base available to leaders and is the most commonly overlooked unintended consequence of this complex change.

Learning about change is not the same as leading change. In fact, it may not be possible to really learn change, without leading change.

I had my first opportunity to lead a major change initiative as the newly appointed president and CEO of EFMA, where I'd faced a grasshopper moment and gained better perspective on that season of my leadership journey. My predecessor and a board sub-committee had already invested significant energy to explore possible changes. Then my appointment came with a mandate to develop a specific change agenda and lead the association forward.

I was excited about this opportunity. But I had no idea what I was getting into.

Over the next eighteen months, we changed the vision, mission, core values, constitution, by-laws, and name of our organization. Yes, you read that right. All those changes happened in the first eighteen months. Once the process began, it was like an avalanche we couldn't stop. I prayed it wouldn't bury us alive.

We branded our new name, The Mission Exchange, and rolled out major new deliverables for our constituency. The changes were well received despite the rapid pace. I benefited greatly from a wise board and a supportive predecessor.

Though I didn't understand it at the time, all this was a warm-up act, like stretching your muscles before a big race. The most complex change was still five years away.

Before accepting the role as EFMA's president and CEO, I had sought input from several respected mission leaders. The most common feedback I'd heard was about the need for our association to merge with another similar association, the Interdenominational Foreign Mission Association (IFMA). Nearly every leader had told me, "There should only be one mission association in the United States and Canada. These two groups need to merge, but it will *never* happen."

In my first meeting with the leader of IFMA, who had come into his role about six months after I'd started mine, I asked for his perspective on a possible merger. We agreed that if a merger were ever to happen, it would need to come from the bottom up, not the top down. Therefore, we aimed to create an environment that would motivate our respective members to start the conversation.

Over the next four years, we collaborated in every way possible. Within three years, all our major events were jointly sponsored. Our boards started meeting together over a meal on the front end of our flagship annual conference, and a growing number of mission agencies became members of both associations. The bottom-up conversation was beginning to find a voice. Meanwhile, IFMA also changed its name to CrossGlobal Link. Both associations wanted a fresh sense of identity and purpose.

Eventually we formed a task force with representatives from both associations to study the potential of a merger. The difficulties before us became obvious in the first task force meeting. We exposed years of differences and unspoken layers of mistrust just beneath the surface of our progress like subterranean fault lines threatening an earthquake. I feared the merger process wouldn't survive the first meeting.

The joint task force agreed on a framework to document what our preferred future together could look like. Both leaders—I represented The Mission Exchange and my peer represented CrossGlobal Link— individually drafted separate versions of the preferred future document. Once the documents were complete, we presented them to each other and collated our differences before reporting back to the joint task force.

Over the next year, we mapped out a plan that would ask the members of our two associations—with a combined history of 160 years and nearly two hundred member organizations—to vote themselves out of power, eliminate membership structures altogether, agree on a statement of faith, identify a new business model, create a self-perpetuating board of governance, choose a new leader, and integrate the staff members of both organizations. Just reading that list is exhausting. Looking back, it seems crazy, but that was our plan.

In the fall of 2011, at the annual meetings of both associations, courageous mission executives from both groups simultaneously ratified this bold plan. I was asked to serve as president of the newly formed organization, Missio Nexus. My peer, who led the other association prior to the merger, graciously continued as senior vice president.

It was nothing short of a miracle and a reminder to the leaders who had spoken to me about the need for a merger: With God, anything is possible.

The Complexity Principle

Every Leadership Era in the Bible confirms the complexity principle: Leadership is complex, problematic, and filled with risk, which is why good leaders are needed.[25] And, when a situation involves major change, the complexity principle becomes amplified. We see this in the story of Israel's request for a king, which triggers one of the most complex change journeys in the Bible.

On the surface, asking for a king appears to be a failure of

Samuel's plan for leadership succession. But the elders of Israel were not just asking for a new leader. By rejecting theocracy in favor of monarchy, they were asking for a new leadership structure. It is important to understand that even the most positive change never eliminates problems. It merely allows you to exchange your current problems for different problems you have come to believe are preferable.

A primary change-management skill is the ability to anticipate the unintended consequences of change accurately enough to ensure the problems you inherit are indeed preferable. The elders of Israel became intoxicated by the idea of change without any real understanding of what they were asking for. Before exploring how their massive change initiative plays out, consider the context leading up to it.

How Samuel Emerged as a Leader

The last few verses of 1 Samuel 7 form a summary paragraph describing the final twenty-five to thirty years of Samuel's leadership. He served from his home base in Ramah, and "went on a circuit from Bethel to Gilgal to Mizpah, judging Israel in all those places" (1 Sam. 7:16).

The summary paragraph that concludes chapter seven is connected to chapter eight with a description of Samuel's succession plan: "When Samuel grew old, he appointed his sons as judges for Israel" (1 Sam. 8:1). This statement sets up the leadership conversation between Samuel and the elders of Israel about the complex change they requested. But we can't understand a leadership conversation by simply identifying the leader and the followers. We must also understand the situation, which requires rewinding to the beginning of Samuel's story.

Samuel's special birth circumstances are well known to leaders. His mother fulfilled her promise to God by delivering the young boy to Eli, the priest who would become his mentor.

Leadership influence and giftedness should compound over time, converging and building to a crescendo in the final chapters of life.[26] That wasn't Eli's story. He wasn't in tune with God's voice. At the peak of his leadership "the word of the LORD was rare; there were not many visions" (1 Sam. 3:1).

Eli had so little influence at the end of his life that the Israelites didn't consult him before taking the ark of the covenant of God to the front lines of their battle with the Philistines. They treated the ark like a mascot at a pep rally. Eli was powerless to intervene.

The soldiers of Israel received momentary encouragement from the presence of the ark, but they experienced neither the power nor the favor of God. The text tells the sorry state of affairs: "So the Philistines fought, and the Israelites were defeated and every man fled to his tent. The slaughter was very great; Israel lost thirty thousand foot soldiers. The ark of God was captured, and Eli's two sons, Hophni and Phinehas, died" (1 Sam. 4:10-11).

That same day a messenger ran from the battle lines to bring home the bad news. When the messenger told the townspeople, they sent up a cry. Eli heard the uproar, asked what it meant, and was told:

> Israel fled before the Philistines, and the army has suffered heavy losses. Also, your two sons, Hophni and Phinehas, are dead, and the ark of God has been captured (1 Sam. 4:17).

The bad news hit Eli like a gale-force wind. He literally fell backward off his chair, broke his neck, and died.

As if the story couldn't get any worse, Eli's daughter-in-law, the wife of Phinehas, died too. She was pregnant and near the time of delivery when the shock of the tragedy put her into labor, and she died giving birth. The midwife tried to console her with the arrival of her son, but she paid no attention. With her dying breath, Eli's daughter-in-law named the baby Ichabod, which means *no glory,* because "the glory has departed from Israel, for the ark of God has been captured" (1 Sam. 4:22).

Eli, a powerless leader, was dead and his family virtually wiped out. The armies of Israel had suffered heavy losses. Their nation was under siege. The ark of God was in the hands of the Philistines. The glory of God had departed. You'd think this was a country music song in the making.

In the leadership structure of Israel, Samuel was literally the last man standing. This was his introduction to leadership. He was probably about seventeen years old.

Samuel's Twenty Years of Silence

While the glory of God had departed from Israel, the power of God remained visible elsewhere. The Philistines put the Ark of the Covenant in the temple of Dagon and set it beside the idol of their false god. The next day, "there was Dagon, fallen on his face on the ground before the ark of the LORD" (1 Sam. 5:2)! They picked up Dagon and put him back in his place, only to discover the next day that the idol was once again on its face, with its head and hands broken off. Clearly the God of Israel was not like the Philistine idols.

After the Philistines experienced God's power firsthand, they decided it was too hot to handle, so they sent the Ark of the Covenant back to Israel. The Israelites received the ark at Beth Shemesh, only to have two men struck dead after they looked inside it—a severe reminder of God's glory. From there the Israelites moved the ark to the house of Abinidab at Kiriath Jearim and consecrated his son Eleazar to guard it. "It was a long time, twenty years in all, that the ark remained at Kiriath Jearim" (1 Sam. 7:2).

The text skips two decades with no information about what happened during this twenty-year window. Where was Samuel and what was he doing? We know only the outlines. Samuel's farewell speech indicates that he led Israel from his youth (I Sam. 12:2). After the death of Eli and his two sons, the young Samuel went back to his hometown of Ramah, where he began his ministry as a judge over Israel. Eventually he married, had children, and served Israel with integrity.[27] Samuel became a model leader, resisting the temptation to abuse his power for selfish gain. As an old man, reflecting on his life, Samuel asked the people:

> Whose ox have I taken? Whose donkey have I taken? Whom have I cheated? Whom have I oppressed? From whose hand have I accepted a bribe to make me shut my eyes? If I have done any of these, I will make it right. (1 Sam. 12:3)

The people responded to Samuel, "You have not cheated or oppressed us" (1 Sam. 12:4).

Samuel's faithful service and effective leadership during these twenty-years of silence won the respect of the people. When the burden of Philistine rule grew heavy, the Israelites sought the Lord and turned to Samuel for counsel. By this time, Samuel was about thirty-seven years old. He exhorted the people to show their sincerity by putting away their idols and repenting of their sin. The people gathered at Mizpah for a sacred assembly where Samuel interceded for them.

In response to Samuel's plea, God gave Israel victory by using loud thunder to stir panic among the Philistines and make them vulnerable to routing by the Israelites. Samuel then led the Israelites in acknowledging the Lord's help. His position as Israel's leader was solidified, and throughout his lifetime as "the hand of the LORD was against the Philistines" (1 Sam. 7:13).

Samuel continued as leader and judge over the people from his home base in Ramah for the rest of his life. When he grew old, he appointed his sons as judges in his place over Israel. "But his sons did not walk in his ways. They turned aside after dishonest gain and accepted bribes and perverted justice" (1 Sam. 8:3). The leadership succession plan failed, and in this context, the people asked for a king.

Succession Planning vs. Organizational Development

The elders of Israel came as a group to Samuel's home base at Ramah with a unified voice to ask for a king. They rejected Samuel's sons as their leaders and instead asked for a totally new leadership structure. Note the difference: Asking for a new leader is succession planning, but asking for a new leadership structure is organizational development. Both represent important change initiatives, but the change in structure is much more complex.

Samuel took their request personally as a rejection of him. But God spoke to Samuel, saying, " ... it is not you they have rejected, but they have rejected me as their king" (1 Sam. 8:7). In doing so, the leaders were asking for a remake of the organizational structure, from the theocracy of a divine king represented in the priesthood, to the monarchy of a human king.

Building a new leadership structure is much more complex than finding a new leader because it is difficult to anticipate the unintended consequences of structural change. This is why God instructed Moses to "warn them solemnly and let them know what the king who will rule over them will do" (1 Sam. 8:9).

As stated earlier, even the most positive change initiative doesn't eliminate problems. It merely allows us to exchange our current problems for new problems we have come to believe are preferable. The judgment call of a change initiative requires leaders to anticipate and articulate the unintended consequences of change. The unintended consequences of complex change can become a high-stakes game of pickup sticks. You pull one stick out of the pile without knowing for sure how it will affect the interconnected sticks.

A Harsh Lesson from Giving People What They Want

God outlined to Samuel some of the key unintended consequences of a change from theocracy to monarchy—none of them good—and instructed him to pass along the information to the leaders of Israel.

Samuel warned them that the king would conscript their sons and daughters—some to serve in a standing army, others to "plow his ground and reap his harvest," and still others "to be perfumers and cooks and bakers" (1 Sam. 8:12–13).

Samuel also warned them that the king would impose taxes by taking "the best of your fields and vineyards and olive groves," along with "a tenth of your grain and your vintage and give them to his officials and attendants" (1 Sam. 8:15). In addition, he said, the king will take "your menservants and maidservants and the best of your cattle and donkeys" and "your flocks" (1 Sam. 8:17). Basically, the king will own you.

Eventually the king would push the boundaries of conscription and taxation to the point where the people themselves would be subjugated as slaves. And when that day came, their cry to the Lord would not be answered.

My father used to say the reason the grass is greener on the other side of the fence is because it's growing on top of the septic system. That's not always true. But it reminds us of the importance of carefully exploring the unintended consequences of change.

Samuel discharged his duty to warn the people. But they refused to listen to him. They persisted in their demand for a king to lead them and go out before them in battle "like all the other nations" (1 Sam. 8:20).

A Radical Change in the Situation

As outlined in the opening chapter, the three basal elements of every leadership interaction are the leader, the followers, and the situation. The situation can be viewed in both a macro and micro context. The macro context for my leadership survey of the Bible is reflected in the four Leadership Eras, Patriarchal, National, Transitional, and Spiritual.

In this chapter, we see how the National Leadership Era subdivides into the pre-kingdom phase of theocracy and the kingdom phase of monarchy. Moving from theocracy to monarchy radically changes the situation. The implied social contract of monarchy defines the expectations followers have of their leaders very differently from that of theocracy. Next, we see what happens when the Israelites' shifting expectations clash with unintended consequences of change— conscription, taxation, and subjugation— which God made known to the leaders of Israel through Samuel.

Corruption is a condition of the human heart, not a function of leadership structure. Under a theocratic leadership structure, Eli's sons, and later Samuel's sons, "turned aside after dishonest gain and accepted bribes and perverted justice" (1 Sam. 8:3). But the leadership structure of the theocracy and the limited power base of spiritual authority restrained the scope and impact of their corruption. The sons of Eli and Samuel could only abuse their power one person at a time, as they received the offerings of the people and resolved disputes as judges.

But when the change from theocracy to monarchy radically redefined the social contract between leaders and followers, it also greatly expanded the power base available to leaders. Monarchy gave leaders access to the threat of force and simultaneously increased the scope and impact of potential corruption.

The subjects of a king expect a standing army (conscription), along with governmental infrastructure (taxation). The army provides the implied threat of force needed to collect taxes. The king has the power to scale the impact of his influence for either good or evil. But a standing army and a taxable population are too often like a strong mixed drink that intoxicates a monarch with too much power. His judgment becomes dulled as his appetites entice him to enslave his people. This is exactly what God warned the leaders of Israel would happen.

Understanding Spiritual Authority

At the heart of leadership is influence. According to Leadership Emergence Theory, the first question we ask after identifying the leader, the followers, and the situation, is: How is the leader trying to gain *influence* with this group of followers in this situation? The leader-follower dynamic swings on influence. When leaders influence followers, they must operate from a specific power base.

Until this point, the influence of Israel's theocratic leaders, such as Moses, Joshua, and Samuel, required spiritual authority. Today, just as in biblical times, followers give their leaders *spiritual authority*, which is the right to influence—based on the followers' perception of the leader's *spirituality*. But followers don't give the leader spirituality; it only comes from a relationship with God. Under Israel's new monarchy, a relationship with God was no longer the most important qualification for leadership.

The transition from theocracy to monarchy expanded the power base available to Israel's leaders. This shift is the most commonly overlooked and unintended consequence of the complex change that occurred during the National Leadership Era.

Spiritual authority is not the *only* form of legitimate power. But it is the *most* important. Effective Christian leaders view spiritual authority as their primary and preferred power-base.[28] They understand the priority of spiritual authority and actively seek a platform for influence flowing from the force and weight of their character, formed through their relationship with God. Here again we are reminded why Samuel Logan Brengle finished well: Because he lived in the overflow of being spiritually saturated for many years by consistent time with God.

Leaders gain spiritual authority by modeling godly character over time, engaging with followers in spiritual experiences and serving them with gifted power.

But leadership is a contact sport. It is complex, problematic, and filled with risk. Remember Joseph, languishing in prison—his reward for refusing to have an affair with Potiphar's wife? Think of the disappointment Moses, Joshua, and Caleb must have felt when the ten spies spread a bad report among the Israelites to keep them from taking the promised land. Or how about young Samuel, beginning his leadership journey after the ark was captured and after Eli and his two sons suddenly died?

Our character as leaders is refined as we walk with God through difficult circumstances and experience his sufficiency to meet us at our point of need. We come to know God, but not in a textbook way. We come to real-life knowledge of God through deep experiences with him, which develop our spirituality and thereby establish our spiritual authority. Over time, followers recognize the godly character he forms in us.

Godly leaders don't flaunt their spirituality. But neither do they hide it. One of the ways leaders gain spiritual authority with followers is by engaging with them in spiritual experiences and talking openly about what God is doing in their life. An authentic leadership story reveals struggles and victories. It is possible to lack spiritual authority—not because of a void of spirituality but rather because of a lack of transparency.

Spiritual authority is buttressed when leaders serve with gifted power. This includes, but is not limited to, miracles and the supernatural. Gifted power can be as simple as a teaching ministry marked by the presence of the Holy Spirit or the anointing of God on the ministry of worship.

A Prisoner with Power

The idea of spiritual authority is evidenced most clearly in the theocratic, pre-kingdom sub-phase of the National Leadership Era. The leadership structure of theocracy did not allow for many of the other power bases that would later be exercised under Israel's monarchy. We see glimpses of spiritual authority throughout the Bible, but it resurfaces as the dominant platform for influence in the

Spiritual Leadership Era of the New Testament.

In Paul's leadership experience, we find one of the most compact and dramatic illustrations of spiritual authority in the Bible. After many travels as a missionary, Paul was taken prisoner and put on a ship headed for Rome, where he would stand trial before Caesar. The ship had docked on the island of Crete, where the danger of storms from seasonal weather patterns added risk to the journey.

In this context, Paul wanted to influence both the captain of the ship and the centurion responsible for delivering him to Rome. So he warned them:

> "Men, I can see that our voyage is going to be disastrous and bring great loss to ship and cargo, and to our own lives also." But the centurion, instead of listening to what Paul said, followed the advice of the pilot and the owner of the ship (Acts 27:10-11).

It is not surprising that the centurion relied on the advice of the ship's pilot and owner rather than heeding Paul's words. The island harbor was unsuitable for winter, so the owner decided to sail on. But then the ship encountered storms so violent that the crew threw the cargo overboard. The storm raged for days until they "finally gave up all hope of being saved" (Acts 27:20). The story continues:

> After the men had gone a long time without food, Paul stood up before them and said: "Men, you should have taken my advice not to sail from Crete; then you would have spared yourselves this damage and loss. But now I urge you to keep up your courage, because not one of you will be lost; only the ship will be destroyed. Last night an angel of the God whose I am and whom I serve stood beside me and said, 'Do not be afraid, Paul. You must stand trial before Caesar; and God has graciously given you the lives of all who sail with you.' So keep up your courage, men, for I have faith in God that it will happen just as he told me. Nevertheless, we must run aground on some island" (Acts 27:21–26).

As the storm continued to rage, it drove the ship toward land. The sailors were afraid they would be dashed against the rocks so "they dropped four anchors from the stern and prayed for daylight"

(Acts 27:29). Several sailors decided to make a run for it and let down the lifeboat while pretending to lower anchors into the sea. Paul saw through their plan and told the centurion and his soldiers, "Unless these men stay with the ship, you cannot be saved" (Acts 27:31). Based on that simple statement, the soldiers cut the ropes on the lifeboat and let it fall into the sea.

In the midst of this panic and chaos, Paul spoke once again to his fellow travelers, reminding them they had gone without food for nearly two weeks. He urged them to eat and asserted with confidence: "Not one of you will lose a single hair from his head" (Acts 27:34). He then prayed, broke bread, and began to eat. Encouraged by his example, the rest of the men began to eat too.

At daybreak, the sailors ran the ship aground, and the stern was broken to pieces by the storm. The soldiers wanted to kill all the prisoners to prevent attempts to escape. But the centurion wanted to spare Paul's life, so he intervened by instructing everyone to jump overboard and head ashore.

They landed on the island called Malta as the cold, rainy weather continued. The islanders showed unusual kindness by building a fire for warmth. As Paul reached down to put more wood on the fire, a poisonous snake fastened itself to his hand. The islanders assumed Paul to be an evil man who, though escaping from the raging sea, was now getting his due. "But Paul shook the snake off into the fire and suffered no ill effects" (Acts 28:5).

Seeing this, the chief official of the island welcomed Paul into his home and showed great hospitality. Paul soon learned that the chief official's father was sick in bed, suffering from fever and dysentery. Paul went in to visit him and, "after prayer, placed his hands on him and healed him" (Acts 28:8). When word circulated about the healing of the chief official's father, others brought their sick family members and friends to Paul to be cured. The islanders honored Paul and his entourage in many ways, and when it was time to sail on, they furnished the group with supplies.

This story provides one of the clearest examples of spiritual authority in the Bible. Paul wanted to influence the ship's captain and the centurion before they sailed from Crete. But as a prisoner he appeared to have no power base from which to operate as a leader. Even so, Paul modeled godly character. He influenced his captors by showing poise and calm while they were paralyzed by fear.

Paul engaged the men on the ship in a spiritual experience as he explained to them the angel's message and assured them they would be saved. When the sailors tried to escape on the lifeboat, Paul's spiritual authority had already been established. A simple one-sentence warning caused the centurion to cut the rope and release the lifeboat into the sea.

The evidence of God's power—both in preserving Paul's life after he was bitten by the snake and in fulfilling Paul's prayer for healing of the chief official's father—solidified Paul's platform for influence. He was still a prisoner when the group left Malta. But he was the most influential person among the 276 people on the boat, operating exclusively from a power base of spiritual authority.

Leading Change with Spiritual Authority

Effective change-management calls for a diverse set of leadership skills. The ability to envision what could be, and translate the dream into the manageable steps of a plan, must be combined with persuasive communication skills. Add to this the discipline of execution and the flexibility to adapt. Even the best plans need to be modified when they collide with reality.

Spiritual authority does not replace other tools in a leader's change-management toolbox. But leading change, especially complex change, from a power base of spiritual authority lowers the resistance of followers. Spiritual authority is to leading change what oil is to an engine. It lubricates the process, reduces the friction, and prevents the situation from overheating.

All change forces us as leaders, and our followers, to confront uncertainty as we move from what is to what could be—from our current set of problems to new ones we believe we'll like better. The resistance of followers to the uncertainty of change can be organized into four categories: fear, timing, confusion, and attack.[29]

Every seasoned leader attempting to initiate change has heard followers respond by saying, *If we do that I'm afraid....* You can probably complete this sentence with more than one example.

Fear is powerful. And most of us have a library full of memories that reinforce just about any fear. Not all fear is irrational. But it triggers emotions and complicates the conversation. Emotional responses are rarely overcome by logical reasons.

Timing is critical for major change. A good idea at the wrong time is a bad idea. Perhaps that's why delay is such a widespread tactic for resisting change. Playing the timing card allows for passive resistance. In some cases, the resistance is actually presented as support. *Your idea has a lot of merit, but I don't think we're ready for it.* The delay tactic democratizes resistance to change because it doesn't require carefully thought-out positions or professional expertise on the issue at hand.

Wise leaders welcome robust conversation about the implications of change. That's how unintended consequences are often identified. But there is a difference between exploring second- or third-order consequences and using confusion as a smoke screen to derail a change initiative.

If we take this course of action, I'm not sure how it will affect _____ (fill in the blank). Sometimes confusion is supported with detailed projection. People may torture the data to get it to say whatever they want.

Other times, resistance to change has nothing to do with the idea itself. Why shoot at the idea when you can ridicule the person presenting it? When change-resisters go into attack mode, they may make subtle references to a lack of competency or preparedness. Attack can also devolve into outright condemnation of character and values, which can bring out the worst in leaders. There is wisdom in the old saying: *Never wrestle with a pig. You'll both get dirty. And the pig likes it.*

Spiritual authority fuels trust, and trust is essential for leaders seeking to help followers overcome the most common barriers to change. High-trust relationships overcome fear, break through confusion, muster courage, and maintain unity. The more complex the change, the greater the uncertainty and the greater the need for trust. Trust is like air; when it's present we don't even think about it. When it's absent we can't think about anything else.

Godly Character in the Face of Failure

Samuel's sons did not walk in his ways, so the people of Israel were no longer willing to give them the right to influence. They lost their spiritual authority and had no other platform for influence under theocracy. This situation brought the elders of Israel to Samuel, asking for a complex change they didn't fully understand.

Most scholars agree God's ultimate plan for Israel included an eventual transition from theocracy to monarchy. We don't know what an ideal change journey would have looked like because the elders of Israel pressed the issue on their own ill-advised terms. Moving beyond leadership succession to a new leadership structure had game-changing implications.

Spiritual authority, the primary power base in a theocracy, would become an optional power base in a monarchy. The biblical kings who stand out for their accomplishments as effective leaders are those who, when leading at their best, operated from a power base of spiritual authority.

Moses lived a godly life, experienced intimacy with God, and performed some of the most amazing miracles recorded in the Bible. Yet even with the help of Joshua and Caleb, he couldn't convince the Israelites to take the Promised Land they confirmed was flowing with milk and honey.

There are no guarantees. Change will always be part of leadership. And leadership will always be complex, problematic, and filled with risk. That's why some change initiatives will fail. Regardless of the outcome, spiritual authority will always be the preferred power base, and leaders who operate from this platform can reflect godly character even in the face of failure.

CHAPTER 04

Failure

Failure

NATIONAL
LEADERSHIP ERA

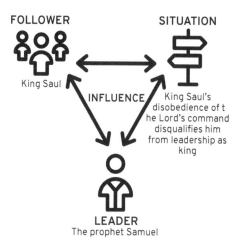

FOLLOWER

King Saul

SITUATION

INFLUENCE

King Saul's disobedience of t he Lord's command disqualifies him from leadership as king

LEADER
The prophet Samuel

"You acted foolishly," Samuel said. "You have not kept the command of the LORD that your God gave you; if you had, he would have established your kingdom over Israel for all time. But now your kingdom will not endure." —1 Samuel 13:13–14

Executive Summary

Leaders experience various kinds of failure and can learn from it. There are qualifying failures, and disqualifying failures. These can be further subdivided into character-based failure, and competency-based failure. Disqualifying, character-based failure can be partial or complete. Competency-based failure can be direct or indirect. Some failure is so costly that wise leaders will seek to learn vicariously through the failure of others. King Saul is the prototype for character-based, disqualifying failure. His life calls out to us for vicarious learning. The best way to avoid the leadership pitfalls of disqualifying failure is to become laser-focused on finishing well.

Before he became king of Israel, David spent a lot of time in the fields, tending sheep. I imagine him lying on the ground, looking up into the night sky, and finding inspiration for a worship song: "The heavens declare the glory of God; the skies proclaim the work of his hands" (Ps. 19:1).

What David never imagined is the close-up view we now have of the farthest corners of galaxies, thanks in part to the Hubble Telescope. Named after astronomer Edwin Hubble, it is the first major optical telescope placed in low Earth orbit, above the haze of the atmosphere, rain clouds, and light pollution. Search the Internet for Hubble Telescope images, and see for yourself what David described as the glorious work of God's hands. It's breathtaking.

But that's not how the Hubble story began.

On April 23, 1990, *Nightline* anchor Ted Koppel interviewed Charles Pellerin, NASA's director of astrophysics. It was the evening before the shuttle launch to deploy the Hubble telescope. The interview explored a variety of questions. Could NASA's budget be put to better use on social programs? What can we expect to discover? How will this impact the average person? All these questions led to what the waiting world ultimately wanted to know: Will it work?

Charles Pellerin praised his team, explained how rigorously they had tested the shuttle, and affirmed his answer, "It will!"

The following day after a textbook-perfect launch, the telescope deployed, powered up, and achieved initial communication with the ground. In a high-flying grand opening, the aperture for the Hubble telescope was opened to let starlight in. When a fuzzy spot of light appeared on the monitors, everyone breathed a sigh of relief. The team had intentionally deployed the telescope out of focus.

Everything was going exactly as planned. In fact, everything went so well that Charles Pellerin decided to visit his colleagues in Japan. He was out of touch for a week. Remember, this was 1990, long before everyone had a mobile phone and checked email every few minutes.

Pellerin flew back from Japan thinking about the Rose Garden at the White House, where a celebration would probably be on the schedule to honor him for the work on the Hubble telescope. He called his secretary from the flight club at the St. Louis airport and was immediately transferred to Len Fisk, his boss at NASA. Pellerin recounts the conversation like this:

"Charlie, where are you?"
"I'm in St. Louis, but I'll be back in Washington tonight."

"I'm glad to hear that. Charlie, what do you know about spherical aberration?"

"I know that it is a common mistake by amateurs. They sometimes make mirrors with a 'down-edge.' A telescope with a spherically aberrated mirror is useless."

Fisk got more specific: "What would you say if I told you we launched Hubble with a spherically aberrated mirror?"

"I would say you are annoyed that I had a good time in Japan, while you had to tend to the Washington bureaucracy. This is a really bad joke."

"Ok. Put the phone down, but don't hang up. Just find the front page of any newspaper and bring it back."

Charles Pellerin grabbed a copy of the *St. Louis Post-Dispatch,* and looked at the cover. The headline read, "National Disaster, Hubble Launched With Flawed Mirror."

Then he responded to Fisk: "You guys are really something. How did you plant a fake newspaper in here?"

Of course it wasn't fake. The flawed mirror meant NASA had sent $1.7 billion of taxpayer money into space, the literal opposite and figurative equivalent of flushing money down the toilet.

Charles Pellerin and his colleagues faced one of the most expensive and publicly exposed failure moments in history. Congressional committees held public hearings designed as much to humiliate as to investigate.

After a week of testimony, Pellerin needed an escape. He went with a friend to a Judy Collins concert outside of town. When she walked on stage, her main microphone didn't work. She went to another microphone and said, "Aren't you glad the idiots that built the Hubble telescope didn't build this sound system. At least we have a backup."[30]

That's when you know you have a famous failure.

Leadership is filled with risk. We say failure is not an option. But regardless, if you are a leader, failure *is* an option. Thankfully, few will ever experience a failure as costly or public as the initial launch of the Hubble telescope.

As we'll see in biblical conversations explored in this chapter, leaders experience various kinds of failure and can learn from it. But some failure is so costly that wise leaders will seek to learn vicariously through the failure of others, in order to avoid repeating devastating mistakes.

For example, King Saul's leadership began at a high-risk moment. The complex change journey from theocracy to monarchy meant everything was new for everyone. Israel had her first king, but almost no royal infrastructure. Her people had no history or generational loyalty to provide a foundation for Saul's leadership.

There was only a hint of a standing army, and because of the oppression of the Philistines, the soldiers had no weapons. The army couldn't be viewed as a serious combat force. Saul had no formal advisors apart from Samuel, no royal city, no taxation system, and no formal judicial process outside the Mosaic law and the priesthood. This is leadership on the heels of the complex change triggered by the demand for a king.

But Saul didn't have to fail. One foolish and untimely act kept his kingdom from being established "over Israel for all time" (1 Sam. 13:13). Among four categories of failure, King Saul's choices led him to disqualifying failure that diminished his leadership and his legacy.

Four Categories of Failure

Heavyweight champion boxer Mike Tyson said, "Everyone has a plan until they get punched in the mouth." Leaders know what it's like to get punched in the mouth. We develop strategies only to discover, upon implementation, that not everything goes according to plan. Failure is both inescapable and unequal. Every leader makes mistakes and ordinary errors in judgment. The failure explored in this chapter is limited to situations where action, or the failure to take action, produces serious consequences for the leader and perhaps also for the followers.

It can be helpful to think about four categories of failure[31]. There are qualifying failures, and disqualifying failures. These can be further subdivided into character-based failure, and competency-based failure. Disqualifying, character-based failure can be partial or complete. Competency-based failure can be direct or indirect. Each category of failure comes with its own kind of consequences.

Failure Tree

Character-Based Qualifying Failure

Leaders who experience character-based qualifying failure make bad choices that interrupt their leadership journey. The fallout of these choices gives leaders the opportunity to grow through brokenness, increased self-awareness, and humble dependence on God. In other words, this kind of failure can actually qualify the leader for even greater leadership, but only if the lessons of failure are learned and applied.

Moses experienced a character-based, qualifying failure when he took matters into his own hands as he attempted to deliver the Israelites from Egypt: "Moses thought that his own people would realize that God was using him to rescue them, but they did not" (Acts 7:25). He fled to the desert, where he settled as a foreigner and started a family. It was forty years before God appeared to Moses in the burning bush and re-engaged his calling to deliver Israel.

Competency-Based Qualifying Failure

Qualifying failure can also be competency-based. This occurs when people are placed in a leadership role for which they are unqualified, and the requirements of the role are simply more than they can handle. Competency-based failure is *direct* when the leader is unable to rise to the challenge of the role. It is *indirect* when a person serving under the leader fails, but the implications of the failure reflect on the leader and affect the entire group. When we say, *the buck stops here,* we are describing the indirect responsibility top leaders have for the actions of those serving under them.

King Rehoboam experienced a qualifying, competency-based failure, after the death of his father, King Solomon.[32] The people of Israel came to Rehoboam, asking for relief from the heavy yoke Solomon had put on them. Rehoboam rejected the counsel of the elders and instead relied on the bad advice of the young men who had grown up with him. He doubled down on the oppression of the people:

> My little finger is thicker than my father's waist. My father laid on you a heavy yoke; I will make it even heavier. My father scourged you with whips; I will scourge you with scorpions (1 Kings 12:10-11).

After the people rejected Rehoboam, his kingdom was eventually divided. His leadership failure cost him greatly.

We see competency-based qualifying failure in the life of Moses too—on top of his character-based failure. But his competency-based failure was indirect. When the ten spies convinced the people not to take the land God had promised them, Moses was ultimately accountable for their actions because he had selected them and sent them into the land. He didn't agree with their conclusion, but was forced to live with and lead through the consequences of their direct failure to take the Promised Land.

Character-Based and Competency-Based Disqualifying Failure

The biblical narrative on failure is dominated by character-based disqualification of leaders. This failure can be *partial,* where the leader is not immediately removed, but future potential is curtailed. Or this failure can be *complete,* where the leader is removed and set aside.

I have found no biblical examples of leaders who were completely disqualified for *competency-based* failure. But this doesn't give us license for mediocre service. Rather it gives us hope for opportunities to learn from our mistakes.[33]

Moses experienced a partial, character-based, disqualifying failure when he disobeyed God by striking the rock with his staff instead of speaking to the rock as he had been commanded. God had told Moses:

> Speak to that rock before their eyes and it will pour
> out its water. You will bring water out of the rock
> for the community so they and their livestock
> can drink (Num. 20:8).

This one act of disobedience—striking instead of speaking—kept Moses from entering the Promised Land with the Israelites after forty years of wandering in the desert. Moses's disobedience serves as a warning and reminder. God holds leaders to a higher standard of accountability. From everyone who has been given much, much will be required (Luke 12:48).

King Saul also learned the lesson of heightened leadership accountability from a character-based disqualifying failure.

Leading in the Aftermath of Complex Change

It is likely that Samuel's farewell address (1 Sam. 12), took place on the first anniversary of King Saul's coronation. In this final message, Samuel emphasized how wrong the Israelites were to ask for a king, saying, "And you will realize what an evil thing you did in the eyes of the LORD when you asked for a king" (1 Sam. 12:17). Saul was present when this speech was given, and had to be questioning his position as king after hearing it.

The Lord sent thunder and rain to supernaturally endorse Samuel's words (1 Sam. 12:18). In fear, the people acknowledged their mistake and appealed to Samuel:

> Pray to the LORD your God for your servants so that we will not die, for we have added to all our other sins the evil of asking for a king (1 Sam. 12:19).

Try to imagine what Saul must have been thinking when he was listening to all this. What would be going through your mind? It can't be the one-year anniversary celebration he envisioned!

Saul's Disqualifying Failure

King Saul is the prototype for character-based, disqualifying failure. His heart-wrenching story gives leaders an opportunity for vicarious learning.

In the biblical text, the setting of this leadership conversation is not entirely clear. Some numbers have been dropped from 1 Samuel 13:1 in the original manuscripts, making the verse difficult to understand. In the Hebrew it reads, "Saul was years old when he became king and he reigned over Israel two years."

Scholars have suggested a more sensible rendering of the verse would be: "Saul was [40] years old when he became king and reigned over Israel [forty-]two years." Yet even this rendering is problematic because Saul was described as a "young" man when he became king. But his son Jonathan was old enough to be in the army at the time—at least twenty years old. This discrepancy might be due to the word translated "young," which can also be translated "choice." Therefore, Saul may have been old enough to have a grown son when he became king.

Saul had solidified his leadership as king over Israel by stepping up against the Ammonite threat that surfaced during the first year of his reign (1 Sam. 11). Later he faces a new threat—the Philistines—that will plague Israel's kings long after him (1 Sam. 13).

Israel's initial military engagement with the Philistines occurred when Jonathan, not Saul, attacked their outpost at Geba. Either Jonathan's actions were unauthorized or Saul was woefully unprepared. Saul responded to news of the attack by sounding the trumpet and summoning his army. Troops were instructed to meet at Gilgal, a place of great significance for Israel and Saul.

God gave the name Gilgal to this place through Joshua, when

Israel had camped there on the plains of Jericho, after crossing the Jordan River. At Gilgal the Israelites had been circumcised, had eaten food from the land after the manna stopped, and had celebrated Passover for the first time in the Promised Land.

Samuel told Saul to meet him in Gilgal after pouring a flask of oil on Saul's head to anoint him the first king of Israel. Samuel's instructions were to "wait seven days until I come to you and tell you what you are to do" (1 Sam. 10:8). Jewish historians say this was a standing rule for Saul in times of crisis: Go to Gilgal and wait for seven days until Samuel arrives to offer sacrifices and give instructions.

After Jonathan led the attack at Geba, the standing rule took effect:

> Saul had the trumpet blown throughout the land and said, "Let the Hebrews hear!"... And the people were summoned to join Saul at Gilgal (1 Sam. 13:3–4).

Then Saul's seven-day waiting period began. With the rule came an extremely difficult leadership challenge in this particular case. Circumstances had spiraled out of his control, triggered by Jonathan's unauthorized attack on the Philistines. Saul was woefully outmanned, with only three thousand men to fight against the Philistine army of three thousand chariots, six thousand charioteers, and "soldiers as numerous as the sand on the seashore" (1 Sam. 13:5).

It is easy to see the folly in Saul's actions from hindsight. But put yourself inside his head for a moment. Your army is under-resourced; the text says "not a soldier with Saul and Jonathan had a sword or spear in his hand" (1 Sam. 13:22). Your troops are in total chaos. Morale is at the lowest possible point. Most of the soldiers are deserting; only six hundred remain (1 Sam. 13:15). Those who stay with you are quaking with fear and hiding in caves, behind bushes, and in cisterns. And the expected arrival of Samuel has not occurred as the time ticks down to the final moments on the seventh day (1 Sam. 13:7–8).

What would your leadership instincts tell you to do?

Saul felt compelled to act. Just as you or any leader probably would. He had to do something to inspire his beleaguered troops and infuse hope into a hopeless situation.

But instead of demonstrating his dependence on God, Saul's actions showed just the opposite. And the timing could not have been worse, right before Samuel arrived.

Saul's Trust Wait

Why did God establish a standing rule for Saul to wait at Gilgal for seven days until Samuel arrived to offer sacrifices and give instructions? Nowhere in the Bible do we see any indication of any other leader given these instructions.

I'm sure you are familiar with the team-building exercise known as the *trust fall*. In this exercise, one person is blindfolded and asked to fall backward while trusting her team members to break her fall. The seven-day period in Gilgal was a *trust wait* for Saul. God was administering an obedience test by exposing Saul's need to trust God. Saul was found wanting, although only by a matter of minutes. Nonetheless, he failed the test.

In his impatience, Saul stepped outside the boundaries of his office as king. He did what only the priests should do: He officiated the burnt offering and the fellowship offering. Then, "just as he finished making the offering, Samuel arrived" (1 Sam. 13:10). How many times do you think Saul regretted his inability to wait a few more minutes?

Samuel's words to Saul dripped with consequences:

> What have you done? You have acted foolishly....
> Now your kingdom will not endure; the LORD has
> sought out a man after his own heart and appointed
> him leader of his people, because you have not kept
> the Lord's command (1 Sam. 13:11, 13–14).

Moving Beyond the Fallout of Failure

When leaders experience significant failure, they lose confidence. And when they lose confidence, their insecurity gains the upper hand. Their internal leadership identity seesaws. They try to counter insecurity with false confidence, bragging about what they've done or who they know. You've likely been around leaders who have done this, because everyone is tempted to do this at one time or another. The seesaw tendency is easy to spot and annoying to be around. When leaders overcompensate, followers and fellow leaders can see it happening.

The pairing of lower confidence and higher insecurity creates a negative feedback loop. When insecure leaders act in false confidence, they are likely to experience more failure, which in turn lowers their confidence and fuels even greater insecurity. You see where this is going. But here's the bigger problem. Insecurity in the life of a leader undermines loyalty in the life of a follower. Let that sink in for a moment. The leader's insecurity undermines the very followers who *want* to support the leader. This irony plays out vividly in Saul's life.

Saul's disqualifying failure reaches its lowest point when he failed to follow clear instructions to destroy the Amalekites. Saul justified his actions by explaining they were simply bringing the best of the plunder to Gilgal, where Samuel could offer them as sacrifices to God (1 Sam. 15:20-21).

Samuel rebuked Saul, explaining that obedience is better than sacrifice. The excuse for Saul's disobedience is telling: "I was afraid of the people and so I gave in to them" (1 Sam. 15:24). In other words, he had low confidence and high insecurity.

In the following chapters of Samuel's narrative, David enters the story as the "man after God's own heart," of whom Samuel had spoken when explaining to Saul that his kingdom would not endure. David was brave and loyal. He did more than kill Goliath. The text says, "whatever Saul sent him to do, David did it so successfully that Saul gave him a high rank in the army" (1 Sam. 18:5). Saul's officers and the people were pleased with David's faithful service.

Instead of celebrating David's victory and loyalty, Saul fed his own insecurity by asking himself: "'What more can he get but the kingdom?' And from that time on Saul kept a jealous eye on David" (1 Sam. 18:9). This was Saul's version of keeping your friends close and your enemies closer.

Yet David's loyalty to Saul never wavered. David refused to kill Saul when given the chance, even though Saul had repeatedly tried to kill him. When Saul and Jonathan died, David and his men "wept and fasted till evening" (2 Sam. 1:12). David wrote a lament for Saul and Jonathan and ordered that the men of Judah be taught to sing it (2 Sam. 1:17).

In the lament, David said of Saul:

> O daughters of Israel, weep for Saul, who clothed you
> in scarlet and finery, who adorned your garments with
> ornaments of gold (2 Sam. 1:24).

Would you write a song like this about the man who chased you like a wild dog, forced you into hiding, and repeatedly tried to kill you? I don't think I would.

Saul's insecurity didn't allow him to benefit from David's loyalty. But contrast Saul with his son Jonathan—the person who had the most to lose when David became the next king of Israel. From the moment he and David first met, Jonathan "became one in spirit with

David, and loved him as himself" (1 Sam. 18:1).

Jonathan's Confident Leadership

David's bravery didn't threaten Jonathan, who centered his confidence in God, not himself. His God-centered confidence stands in relief against Saul's initial disqualifying failure. When Jonathan was alone with his armor-bearer near a Philistine outpost, he said:

> Come, let's go over to the outpost of those
> uncircumcised fellows. Perhaps the LORD will act
> in our behalf. Nothing can hinder the LORD from
> saving, whether by many or by few (1 Sam. 14:6).

Jonathan's confidence in God gave him security as a leader and reinforced the loyalty of his armor-bearer, who replied: "Go ahead; I am with you in heart and soul" (1 Sam. 14:7).

Keep in mind, Jonathan charged the hill to attack this Philistine outpost around the same time Saul usurped Samuel's priestly role at Gilgal, failed the trust-wait test, and therefore received Samuel's rebuke. Saul's leadership instinct was right; he needed to act. But to rally the six hundred men who remained with him, Saul would have showed better leadership if he had given a speech similar to what Jonathan told his armor-bearer.

What if Saul had gathered his men and spoken to them of his confidence in God? He could have said: *Samuel has promised to come, and I believe he will. I know we are outnumbered. We have no weapons. There is no way we can stand against the Philistine army in our own strength. But nothing can hinder the Lord from saving, whether by many or by few.*

According to Samuel's words, God would have established Saul's kingdom over Israel for all time (1 Sam. 13:13). But Saul's failure cost him that opportunity.

David's Second-Generation Loyalty

After David's anointing as king, he consolidated his rule over all Israel in Jerusalem and set up the systems of a mature monarchy. He put in place a commander over his army, an official recorder, a secretary, priests, and royal advisors (2 Sam. 8:15–18). He "reigned over all Israel, doing what was just and right for all his people" (2 Sam. 8:15).

Then David asked the leaders around him a question that can only be understood in the context of his loyal friendship with Jonathan:

"Is there anyone still left of the house of Saul to whom I can show kindness for Jonathan's sake" (2 Sam. 9:1)? The answer turned out to be *yes*. Jonathan had a crippled son named Mephibosheth, who was brought to King David.

When word came to Mephibosheth that David had summoned him, the natural reaction would be to fear the worst. When Mephibosheth arrived, the look on his face must have suggested fear, because David began by telling him not to be afraid. David went on to say:

> I will surely show you kindness for the sake of your father Jonathan. I will restore to you all the land that belonged to your grandfather Saul, and you will always eat at my table (2 Sam. 9:7).

David's friendship with Jonathan shows how loyalty pays dividends over time. But acts of disloyalty flowing from insecurity can also affect the leadership culture and undermine teamwork years later. Unresolved failure brings confidence down and insecurity up. Insecurity in leaders undermines loyalty in followers.

Learning, Not Losing, from Failure

Innovative leaders understand how failure can unlock a treasure trove of good ideas. This upside of failure is why leaders on the steep side of the learning curve urge their followers to fail faster. When you understand that failing faster equates to learning faster, the more grave failure is not failing enough, and therefore not learning. The business world is full of breakthrough products that came from failed experiments.

But keep in mind, it may be well and good to risk a competency-based qualifying failure on the way to improving a product or disrupting a business model. The stakes are exponentially higher with character-based failures. Character lessons are far too costly to learn on our own. My grandfather used to say, "Experience is the best teacher, but if you can learn any other way, do it." This wisdom is especially true for character-based, disqualifying failure.

The only way to win, and not lose, from disqualifying failure is to study the lives of others and learn from their mistakes. We can learn from leaders like Saul whose story ended badly, and from leaders like Daniel who persevered faithfully through difficult circumstances. This is how Samuel Logan Brengle finished well. He spent a lifetime learning from leaders in the Bible who continued to inspire him, even in the final days of his life.

The job-search website, Monster.com, worked with an ad agency for a parody commercial to use in the high-stakes environment of the Super Bowl. The commercial, shot in black and white and supported by an uplifting choral music bed, featured middle school kids delivering the following dialogue:

> Boy: "When I grow up I want to be..."
>
> Girl: "When I grow up, I want to file...all day."
>
> Boy: "I want to claw my way up to middle management."
>
> Girl: "... Be replaced on a whim."
>
> Girl: "I want to be a brown nose."
>
> Boy: "Yes man ..."
>
> Girl: "Yes woman ..."
>
> Boy: "Yes sir ... coming sir."
>
> Boy: "Anything for a raise, sir."
>
> Boy: "When I grow up, I want to be under-appreciated."
>
> Girl: "... be paid less for the same job."
>
> Boy: "I want to be forced into early retirement."
>
> End frame: "What do you want to be?"

The genius of this commercial is the tension it creates in the mind of the viewer. Middle school kids don't dream of a future as a *yes* man or woman in middle management—waiting to be replaced on a whim. But this happens to people all the time.

Leaders don't begin their journey with the dream of becoming a falling star and losing their platform for influence because of infidelity, abuse of power, or embezzlement of resources. Neither do they imagine a day when, at the peak of their potential, they simply stop growing, ignore their family until it falls apart, or read too much of their own press until pride wins the day.

But leaders fall to these kinds of disqualifying failures every day. The most dangerous lie any of us could ever embrace is, *It could never happen to me.*

Five Characteristics of Leaders Who Finish Well

As referenced in chapter two, the widely cited research by Bobby Clinton highlights the challenges of finishing well. Of approximately one hundred biblical leaders about whom we have enough data to study, a sobering minority of one in three finished well.

Leaders who finish well have a vibrant relationship with God right up to the end of their life. They actively develop their God-given potential and seek to grow their capacity over time. And they leave behind some form of ultimate contribution as a testimony to a lifetime of faithful service. The ultimate contribution could be a life worth emulating, a breakthrough idea, or an organization that adds value to others for the sake of God's kingdom.

Daniel stands out as an ideal role model for persevering to the end. His life powerfully illustrates five characteristics that increase the odds of finishing well.

An Impactful Network

Leaders who finish well build a network of people who significantly impact their lives. Leadership is not an individual sport. But the higher we go in leadership the harder we must work to sustain a network of life-giving and authentic relationships.

Daniel was born into the royal family during the reign of King Josiah (Dan. 1:3). He was a young boy in Jerusalem when Josiah led the nation in a national renewal, driven by the discovery of the Book of the Law in the temple. Another key influencer in Daniel's life, the prophet Jeremiah began his ministry in the thirteenth year of Josiah's reign.

Daniel was taken into captivity in Babylon because he stood out as a future leader in Jerusalem. We don't know if he had direct access to godly leaders like Josiah and Jeremiah, but at the very least, he would have been impacted by their example.

While in Babylon, Daniel developed a close friendship with Hananiah, Mishael, and Azariah. Like Daniel, these three men had also been taken from Jerusalem as captives of King Nebuchadnezzar. Together, the four were enrolled in the special three-year training program to indoctrinate captives as future wise men in service of Babylon. Daniel relied on his three friends for prayer support at a critical moment when Nebuchadnezzar threatened to put all his wise men to death—including Daniel—because none could tell him the meaning of a dream he wouldn't reveal. But because of his strong relational network, Daniel didn't have to face this crisis alone.

A Vibrant Relationship with God

Leaders who finish well enjoy personal intimacy with God and experience repeated times of personal renewal.

The story most closely associated with Daniel is his time in the lion's den. His peers in the leadership of Babylon tricked Nebuchadnezzar into signing a law that forbid prayer to any god or man, except the king. Violators would be thrown into a den of lions. The entire plot against Daniel hinged on the predictability and discipline of his personal time with God. They knew he would pray "just as he had done before," regardless of any decree by the king (Dan. 6:10).

A Purposeful Discipline

Leaders who finish well practice purposeful discipline in the important areas of life.

Daniel's captivity and forced enrollment in the Babylonian leadership program caused a traumatic disruption to his life. It would be easy to understand if he decided not to make an issue of the inner conflict he felt about eating the royal food and wine. But he resolved not to defile himself and negotiated wisely with the official over him. God honored Daniel with favor and good health.

A Positive Learning Attitude

Leaders who finish well maintain a positive learning attitude throughout all of life.

Daniel read a letter from Jeremiah that circulated among the exiles, which explained that their captivity would last seventy years. What he learned triggered immediate action. He realized the time had come for the return to Jerusalem and promptly "turned to the Lord God and pleaded with him in prayer and petition, in fasting and in sackcloth and ashes" (Dan. 9:3). Although this happened in the final stages of Daniel's life, he was still fully engaged with what he learned about the purposes of God.

A Lifetime Perspective

Leaders who finish well keep a lifetime perspective, which enables them to focus. They see present leadership and ministry in the context of a bigger picture.

Daniel's public ministry began when he interpreted King Nebuchadnezzar's dream. God revealed the dream to Daniel during a late-night prayer meeting with his three friends. The interpretation reinforced the big picture of God's plan and his sovereignty over the nations and all of history. Daniel never forgot that lesson. No wonder his favorite name for God was the *Most High*.

Daniel finished well. And not by accident.

Focusing on the Finish, Not the Failure

After the public and expensive failure of the Hubble telescope, Charles Pellerin championed the idea of a repair mission. He enlisted the help of scientists around the world and redirected $60 million from his budget to fund the repair of the flawed mirror.

The fact you can google Hubble telescope images and see the handiwork of God in faraway galaxies reveals a far more favorable ending than the headlines, hearings, and jokes about the launch failure may have led anyone to hope for at the time.

I love the Hubble story because it highlights the tenacity and resilience true leaders have in the face of failure. And regardless of how costly or visible your failure may be, it probably isn't going to be referenced by the lead singer at the next concert you attend.

The first response for leaders walking through character-based failure is repentance of sin. The first response for competency-based failure is acceptance of responsibility. From there, regardless of the context for failure, resilience is key.

The best way to avoid the leadership pitfalls of disqualifying failure is to become laser-focused on finishing well. Every one of the five characteristics of finishing well is within reach for us, as they were for Daniel. (1) Seek out a mentor. (2) Cultivate authentic relationships. (3) Enlist accountability partners. (4) Invite them to ask you about your personal time with God, and what you are doing to keep growing. (5) Process life with them in transparent conversations to help maintain your perspective.

Anyone can do this. Far too few actually do. Let's commit together to beat the odds.

CHAPTER 05

Burden

Burden

NATIONAL
LEADERSHIP ERA

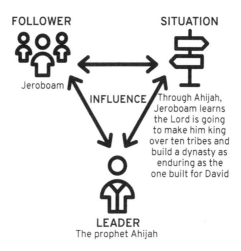

FOLLOWER

Jeroboam

SITUATION

INFLUENCE

Through Ahijah, Jeroboam learns the Lord is going to make him king over ten tribes and build a dynasty as enduring as the one built for David

LEADER
The prophet Ahijah

"I will take you, and you will rule over all that your heart desires; you will be king over Israel. If you do whatever I command you and walk in my ways and do what is right in my eyes ... I will be with you. I will build you a dynasty as enduring as the one I built for David and will give Israel to you." —1 Kings 11:37–38

Executive Summary

Spiritual leaders understand God is the source of both capacity and responsibility for leadership. From that sense of responsibility to God for leadership, we develop a burden for others. Without a sense of responsibility to God for leadership, the others-focused burden often morphs into personal ambition. This is the tragic story of Jeroboam, the first king of the divided kingdom of Israel. The primary evidence of a burden in the heart of a leader is the ministry of intercession for followers. If God has called you to lead a ministry, he has also called you to pray for that ministry.

"Where were you?"

I had been waiting twenty-four hours to ask my dad that question. The tone of my voice had a mixture of irritation and concern. His answer marked me, not just in the moment, but also for life. It revealed a part of my dad's story I hadn't known and a lesson in leadership I'll never forget.

I asked the question the morning after a particularly tense local church board meeting. Parishioners had lined up on different sides of complex issues on the agenda. The situation was already tense before the meeting. As if that weren't enough, my dad went AWOL early in the morning, the day of the meeting. This was long before cell phones so it was much easier to disappear. No one knew where he went or what he was doing.

Everything about the situation seemed out of character for him. I was about two years into my service as an assistant pastor on my dad's church staff and dreaded what his absence might mean for the outcome of the meeting.

As the hours of his disappearance dragged on, my mind started to flirt with worst-case scenarios. It was the missing-person equivalent of losing your keys. You start by looking in the obvious places. When you don't find them, you look again. Anxiety clouds your judgment, and with growing desperation you start looking in places you know you won't find them.

Then, just in time for the meeting, my dad drove into the church parking lot, as if nothing ever happened. He walked into the boardroom and conducted church business as usual.

My first opportunity to debrief the situation was the following morning. I had to find out where he'd been. Our conversation went something like this.

"Dad, where were you?"

In reply, he began to tell me a story: "I was working as a machinist in my twenties when I sensed God calling me to become a pastor. I felt totally inadequate for this role and tried to explain why I wasn't the right person for the job. One day I was walking in the woods, checking my fox traps and wrestling with God about the burden he was giving me for pastoral ministry. I don't recommend this as the best way to get guidance from God. But I thought about the trap least likely to have a fox and said, 'God, if there is a fox in that trap, I'll know you are calling me to become a pastor.' And sure enough, as I got closer to that trap, I could see it had a fox in it. That day, I accepted God's call on my life."

"Dad, that's a really amazing story. But what in the world does it have to do with where you were yesterday?"

"Well, feeling the pressure of everything we're dealing with, and the challenges of the board meeting, I drove to the place where I had set my line of fox traps. I walked into the woods and found the exact spot where that fox had been caught in a trap. And I sat there, next to a tree, all day. I said, 'God, I know that I know, right here in this place, you called me to become a pastor. I told you then I couldn't do it. And you promised to be with me. I still can't do this, and I need a fresh assurance that you will be with me.' God met me there again with the promise he is still with me."

Why Burden Matters

My dad's experiences in the woods—both his initial calling, and the reaffirmation—illustrate important leadership truths. My preferred definition of a leader is someone with God-given capacity and responsibility, who is influencing others toward God's purposes for the group.[34] Spiritual leaders understand God is the source of both capacity and responsibility for leadership. From that sense of responsibility to God for leadership, we develop a burden for others. Because responsibility for my leadership comes from God, my ministry belongs to God. That's liberating, especially when the pressure is on.

Without a sense of responsibility to God for leadership, the others-focused burden often morphs into personal ambition. The position becomes more important than the mission. Leaders who don't understand that capacity and responsibility for leadership come from God are tempted to walk away or take short cuts when the going gets tough. This is the tragic story of Jeroboam, the first king of Israel after the kingdom was divided.

Solomon's Leadership Pipeline

You can't fully appreciate the downfall of Jeroboam until you understand the height from which he fell. We are introduced to him while he is serving as an official in Solomon's workforce (1 Kings 11). All we know of his childhood is that his mother was a widow. He grew up with the challenges of a single-parent home.

We can assume some positive influences on Jeroboam's life because he distinguished himself as a young leader. Jeroboam had been appointed as one of 550 chief officials under King Solomon, in charge of building projects. These officials supervised the workers (1 Kings 9:23). He is described as "a man of standing," which is the same Hebrew phrase the angel of the LORD used to describe

Gideon, as "a mighty warrior" (Judg. 6:12).

We don't know if Solomon inspected the work of his chief officials closely enough to see the potential in Jeroboam, or if others brought the young man to the attention of the king. Regardless, Jeroboam stood out as a young leader worthy of developing. His effective leadership earned him a promotion:

> Now Jeroboam was a man of standing, and when Solomon saw how well the young man did his work, he put him in charge of the whole labor force of the house of Joseph (1 Kings 11:28).

The Could-Have-Been Kingdom

Life was good for Jeroboam. He excelled at work, captured the attention of the king, and received the reward of additional responsibility. He gained status and influence. His mom had to be proud of her son. What could be better than this?

Not long after his promotion, Ahijah the prophet approached Jeroboam on a lonely stretch of road outside Jerusalem. Ahijah ripped the new cloak he was wearing into twelve pieces—a dramatic illustration of a prophetic message:

> Then he said to Jeroboam, "Take ten pieces for yourself, for this is what the LORD, the God of Israel, says: 'See, I am going to tear the kingdom out of Solomon's hand and give you ten tribes.... I will do this because they have forsaken me and worshiped Ashtoreth the goddess of the Sidonians, Chemosh the god of the Ammonites, and have not walked in my ways, nor done what is right in my eyes, nor kept my statutes and laws as David, Solomon's father did'" (1 Kings 11:31–33).

Ahijah went on to say:

> I will take you, and you will rule over all that your heart desires; you will be king over Israel. If you do whatever I command you and walk in my ways and do what is right in my eyes by keeping my statutes and commands, as David my servant did, I will be with you. I will build you a dynasty as enduring as the one I built for David and will give Israel to you (1 Kings 11:37–38).

Jeroboam received a promotion from King Solomon because of his potential and how well he did his work. Now Jeroboam also received a promise from God of a dynasty as enduring as the one built for David. How would you even get your head around that? Along with his God-given capacity as a leader, Jeroboam was given great responsibility for future leadership. But he never realized this amazing potential. Instead of becoming the leader of an enduring Davidic dynasty, Jeroboam became known for the could-have-been kingdom. You've probably never met a family at church who named their newborn son Jeroboam. And there is a reason. He "enticed Israel away from following the LORD and caused them to commit a great sin" (2 Kings 17:21).

Jeroboam became the poster boy for wickedness in Israel. References to the "ways" or "sins" of Jeroboam, or similar derivatives, are used eighteen times in 1 and 2 Kings. He set the benchmark of evil for the kings of Israel who would follow him. When someone wanted to indicate the degree of wickedness of the kings of Israel, they used Jeroboam for comparison. No king scored worse.

Solomon had already received a warning that, because of his disobedience, God would "most certainly tear the kingdom away" from him and give it to one of Solomon's subordinates (1 Kings 11:11). We don't know how Solomon found out about the prophecy spoken by Ahijah, but Solomon tried to kill Jeroboam, who fled to Egypt, where he stayed until he learned of Solomon's death (1 Kings 11:40).

Scripture is silent regarding Jeroboam's time in Egypt. We know from many other biblical accounts that God often uses the detours and delays to shape the character and deepen the calling of a leader. For however long Jeroboam was in Egypt, he had to be thinking often about God's promise of a dynasty as enduring as King David's.

The Would-Have-Been King

Jeroboam rose to leadership of the could-have-been kingdom by displacing Rehoboam, the would-have-been king in line to inherit the throne of a united kingdom from his father Solomon. The people of Israel assembled in Shechem to crown Rehoboam, but when Jeroboam heard about the planned coronation while in exile in Egypt, he returned to Israel. The leaders of Israel's assembly invited Jeroboam to join them in a meeting with Rehoboam before they pledged their allegiance. The leaders put forth grievances about harsh labor under Solomon's rule and asked for assurances of relief in exchange for their loyalty.

Rehoboam's poor handling of this situation became the

competency-based, qualifying failure referenced in chapter four. He doubled down on the harsh treatment of the people, and they walked away, literally, refusing to recognize him as their king. Rehoboam sent out the leader of his labor force to put the people to work, but they stoned the leader to death.

The Israelites called Jeroboam to the assembly of leaders and made him king instead. Only the tribe of Judah remained loyal to Rehoboam, and the house of David. Rehoboam determined to promptly squelch the people's rebellion, so he mustered an army of 180,000 fighting men to march against Jeroboam and reunite the kingdom. But the war effort was aborted when the prophet Shemaiah said to Rehoboam: "Do not go up to fight against your brothers, the Israelites. Go home, every one of you, for this is my doing" (1 Kings 12:24). Rehoboam and his army obeyed the word of the Lord as spoken by the prophet and went home.

Jeroboam was now king of Israel, just as the prophet had spoken. The potential of an enduring dynasty lay before him. He fortified Shechem, the very place Rehoboam had gone to be made king, and established it as his home.

When Ambition Eclipses Burden

Jeroboam had served as a top leader in Solomon's labor force and therefore would have been familiar with the grievances the people brought to Rehoboam about their working conditions. The most logical way for Jeroboam to gain an early political win, and engender loyalty from the people, would have been to quickly and convincingly solve the labor problem.

Pause for a moment to consider that spiritual leaders are not self-made or self-appointed. Their capacity and responsibility for leadership come from God. When leaders connect their responsibility for leadership to God, their attention naturally turns to the followers he has entrusted to them. That sense of responsibility is expressed as a burden the leader carries for others. God never gives leaders a platform for influence for their personal benefit. Rather, God works through leaders to mediate his blessing to followers. Remember the words of Jesus, quoted by Paul to leaders from Ephesus, "It is more blessed to give than to receive" (Acts 20:35). This is the heart of spiritual leadership.

But Israel is no longer a theocracy. By asking for a king to succeed the prophet Samuel, the people had displaced the priority once given to spiritual leadership and had brought unintended consequences upon themselves. Within only a few generations of monarchy, they found themselves asking for relief from harsh labor under Solomon and now Rehoboam.

Despite the seemingly obvious opportunity for a political win, we have no evidence that solving the labor problem even entered Jeroboam's mind. His first thoughts were about his position as king, not about the people or mission God had entrusted to him as the leader of Israel. Jeroboam thought to himself:

> The kingdom will now likely revert to the house of David. If these people go up to offer sacrifices at the temple of the LORD in Jerusalem, they will again give their allegiance to their lord, Rehoboam, king of Judah. They will kill me and return to King Rehoboam (1 Kings 12:26–27).

Leaders without a burden for their followers fixate on what they don't have. They compare their situation with others and project worst-case scenario responses on followers. Rehoboam had one tribe; Jeroboam had ten.[35] But Rehoboam held the territory of Judah, including the capital city of Jerusalem, where his father Solomon built the temple. Jeroboam worried that when the people of Israel went to the temple to worship, their allegiance would return to Rehoboam.

Jeroboam became obsessed by fear of losing what he already had, instead of living by faith in what God had promised to give. David had more faith to believe God for the promise of his future kingship while hiding from Saul than Jeroboam had after already coming to power. Chapter four explored how failure can lead to a loss of confidence and produce insecurity. Jeroboam shows us how fixating on the fear of failure, without actually experiencing it, can bring about the same results. His insecurity resulted in a scarcity mindset that made him vulnerable to bad advice and poor decisions.

Without a burden for their followers, leaders can also become consumed by their own ambition. A God-given burden for others is like a safety rope, protecting leaders from falling into the sinkhole of a prideful preoccupation with success. Jeroboam never attached himself to this safety rope. Leaders gripped by the mission and burdened for their followers will focus on God's purposes for the group. They will sacrifice for the cause, letting go of status and the instinct to survive. They will weep for others more than worrying about themselves. Few leaders modeled this more powerfully than Moses.

Moses's sense of responsibility for leading Israel and the burden he felt for the people was tested repeatedly. After the drain of their constant grumbling and rebellion in the wilderness, God told Moses, "I will strike them down with a plague and destroy them, but I will make you into a nation greater and stronger than they" (Num. 14:12). On the surface this had to be tempting. But Moses instantly resisted God's anger and cried out for mercy on behalf of the people.

Moses shows us a picture of what happens when a sense of responsibility for leadership is rooted and grounded in a burden for followers. He stands in stark contrast to Jeroboam.

Disingenuous Leadership

Jeroboam sought advice regarding his fear that the people would revert their allegiance to Rehoboam if they returned to the temple in Jerusalem to worship God. He received advice to make two golden calves and place them in Dan and Bethel, both located within his territory. He explained to the people, "It is too much for you to go up to Jerusalem. Here are your gods, O Israel, who brought you out of Egypt" (1 Kings 12:28).

Jeroboam's statement, "It is too much for you to go up to Jerusalem," is as close as he ever got to a burden for the people God had entrusted to him. Sadly, nothing about this statement was motivated by concern for his followers. He desperately clutched to his position as king, willing to take shortcuts and make compromises for the sake of self-preservation. Jeroboam had heard the prophecy that God would give him ten tribes after tearing the kingdom from the hand of Solomon, who had forsaken God and allowed the worship of idols.

Somehow, Jeroboam's counselors convinced him God would think differently about the two golden calves than he had about the one built by the people after coming out of Egypt. But Jeroboam's actions were egregious and extreme—so much that it would be easy for leaders today to conclude the lessons of his life don't apply. But leaders take shortcuts and make compromises all the time, driven by the same fear-based motivators. It's alarming to realize the level of self-deception of which leaders are capable when caught in the grip of self-preservation.

Doubling Down on Disobedience

The leadership of Moses and Jeroboam is connected by their opposite response to the idea of a golden calf. The contrast is stark. Moses was burdened for the people. Jeroboam was ambitious for himself.

On both occasions when the golden calf was presented to the

people—during the exodus and by Jeroboam—the exact same words were used: "These are your gods, O Israel, who brought you up out of Egypt" (Ex. 32, 1 Kings 11). During the exodus, when Moses was on Mount Sinai, God made him aware of the people's idolatry. In his anger, God said to Moses, "Now leave me alone so that my anger may burn against them and that I may destroy them. Then I will make you into a great nation" (Ex. 32:10).

But Moses's journey into leadership began with a burden for his people. He had seen an Egyptian beating a Hebrew slave and had taken matters into his own hands by killing the Egyptian. This character-based, qualifying failure sent him into hiding in the desert for forty years. His action was wrong. His burden for the people was right. And that burden is reflected in the way Moses responded when God threatened to destroy the people.

Moses sought God's favor, resisted his anger, and made a plea for mercy. Moses showed concern for God's glory, especially regarding how God would be perceived by the Egyptians, who would assign evil intent to a disastrous show of anger (Ex. 32:12) or who would believe God simply didn't have the power to fulfill the promises he made to their forefathers (Num. 14:16).

The prayer of Moses for the people is a remarkable expression of the burden flowing from his God-given responsibility for leadership:

> Oh, what a great sin these people have committed!
> They have made themselves gods of gold. But now,
> please forgive their sin—but if not, then blot me out
> of the book you have written (Ex. 32:31–32).

Moses reflected the heart of God with a willingness to sacrifice himself on behalf of the people he had been called to lead. It would be noble enough for a leader to sacrifice everything for followers at their best. Moses is ready to do so for Israel at their worst.

Contrast this with Jeroboam. Moses was broken by Israel's sin of worshiping a golden calf. He responded with a willingness to sacrifice everything if God would show the people mercy and forgive them. But Jeroboam doubled down on the same great sin, building two golden calves and enticing the people to worship them—all motivated by self-preservation.

The Prayer Principle

One of the most important leadership lessons from the National Leadership Era is the prayer principle: If God has called you to lead a ministry, he has also called you to intercede for that ministry.[36] Jeroboam never understood the prayer principle.

The primary evidence of a burden in the heart of a leader is the ministry of intercession for followers. Followers most need the prayers of leaders in the moments leaders are most tempted to abandon them. That's what makes Moses's actions so inspiring and challenging. Jesus modeled this principle by praying for his disciples when they were afraid to be associated with him, and deny they knew him (Luke 22:31).

Prayer is like the string on a kite that keeps us tethered to God's heart for the people we lead, as we are carried by the wind of his Spirit. Moses communed with God in the tent of meeting, where the "LORD would speak to Moses face to face, as a man speaks with his friend" (Ex. 33:11). Moses doubled down on intimacy. Jeroboam doubled down on idolatry. Moses was a leader broken by his followers' sin, so he prayed for them. Jeroboam was a leader fearful of losing his followers' loyalty, so he manipulated them. This is what happens to a leader when the position becomes more important than the mission.

Leaders with a heavy burden for their followers, and for the mission that draws them together, will fall to their knees in prayer under the weight of such responsibility. Prayer for followers and for the mission increases the burden, which increases the need for prayer, turning the process into a positive feedback loop. In this sense, the burden from God helps protect leaders from ambition by turning their attention away from themselves toward the needs of others.

Leaders with a burden from God seek divine provision. Leaders without a burden from God seek shortcut solutions. This is the sad and tragic lesson of Jeroboam.

The Sin of Prayerless Leadership

When is it a sin not to pray for someone? Samuel helps us answer that question with his response to the people in his farewell address, "Far be it from me that I should sin against the LORD by failing to pray for you" (1 Sam. 12:23). According to Samuel, it is a sin not to pray for those whom God has given you the responsibility to lead. Samuel emphasized that the failure to pray for the people of Israel would be a "sin against the LORD," not the people. Jesus-following leaders who attempt to lead without prayer flirt with the sin of presumption, assuming God will add his blessing to their human effort.

Leaders *should* pray for other ministries and individuals that do not come under the scope of their leadership. But leaders *must* pray for ministries over which God has placed them. Intercession is the primary evidence of a spiritual burden in the heart of a leader. There is a special responsibility to God as it relates to prayer, which comes with the territory of spiritual leadership.

Here is the paradox of the prayer principle: As the platform for a leader's influence grows in accordance with faithful service, the volume of prayer required to sustain the ministry grows beyond the scope of what the leader can provide. Like Moses on the top of the hill, praying over Joshua and the army of Israel, our "arms grow weary" in prayer and we need the support of others (Ex. 17:11–13). A strong case could be made to suggest the ministry of *every* pastor is beyond this threshold.

When the need for prayer to support a ministry goes beyond what the leader can provide, the only way to fully apply the prayer principle is to recruit other people to pray. This is a leadership function that tests the leader's ability to cast vision and mobilize others. It can be delegated to some extent as the ministry grows, but it always remains a leadership function.

What makes this need even greater is the level of attack against the leader; it often increases in proportion to the growth of the ministry and corresponding platform for influence, making the need for prayer cover increasingly important.

Jeroboam understood the power of prayer firsthand. God sent a prophet to rebuke him for offering sacrifices to the golden calves he had placed in Bethel and Dan. When Jeroboam heard the prophecy against the altar in Bethel he stretched out his hand, pointed at the prophet, and shouted, "Seize him!"

What happened next could leave no doubt in the mind of Jeroboam or anyone who witnessed it: "The hand King Jeroboam stretched out toward the man shriveled up, so that he could not pull it back" (1 Kings 13:4). At this same time, in fulfillment of the words spoken by the prophet, the altar split in two pieces, and its ashes poured out.

After looking at his shriveled hand, Jeroboam spoke to the prophet:

> "Intercede with the LORD your God and pray for me that my hand may be restored." So the man of God interceded with the LORD, and the king's hand was restored and became as it was before (1 Kings 13:6).

It is hard to imagine a more personal and practical way for God to reinforce the power of prayer in Jeroboam's life. And yet:

Even after this, Jeroboam did not change his evil ways, but once more appointed priests for the high places from all sorts of people. Anyone who wanted to become a priest he consecrated for the high places. This was the sin of the house of Jeroboam that led to its downfall and to its destruction from the face of the earth (1 Kings 13:33–34).

Finding Courage to Carry the Burden

God gives leaders a burden, flowing from their sense of responsibility for leadership. The burden helps us stay focused on pursuing the mission instead of holding onto our position. The burden drives us to our knees in prayer, reconnects us with God and his heart for the people he wants to bless through our leadership.

Over a lifetime, we can expect multiple seasons where the challenges of leadership and the burden of the mission will weigh us down. We need personal and timely reassurance from God in these difficult times. All leaders need affirmation. The most important affirmation comes from God.[37]

Divine affirmation reminds us of God's approval and brings a renewed sense of purpose along with a refreshed desire to persevere. This was my father's experience and testimony when facing a difficult season as a local church pastor. He went back to the place where God had originally given him the responsibility for leadership, and God met him with a renewed sense of his divine presence.

Timely affirmation from God to leaders is seen in all four Leadership Eras of the Bible. Those who lean in to the burden of leadership are most likely to experience affirmation from God. The burden Moses felt for the people of Israel drove him to prayer on their behalf. In this challenging season, Moses cried out to God:

> You have been telling me, "Lead these people," but you have not let me know whom you will send with me. God responded to Moses saying, "My presence will go with you, and I will give you rest" (Ex. 33:12–14).

Daniel was burdened for the exiles after reading the letter from Jeremiah, promising God would bring them back to their homeland after seventy years. Daniel responded by pleading with God "in prayer and petition, in fasting, and in sackcloth and ashes" (Dan.

9:3). While Daniel was praying, confessing his sin and the sin of his people, and making his request to God, the angel Gabriel was sent by God with a message of affirmation. Gabriel said to Daniel, "As soon as you began to pray, an answer was given, which I have come to tell you, for you are highly esteemed" (Dan. 9:23).

Jesus was the recipient of divine affirmation at the time of his baptism and on the Mount of Transfiguration (Matt. 3:17, 17:5). On another occasion, Jesus revealed the depth of the burden he was carrying:

> How my heart is troubled, and what shall I say?
> "Father, save me from this hour?" No, it was for this
> very reason I came to this hour. Father, glorify your
> name (John 12:27)!

The Father responded with affirmation: "I have glorified it, and will glorify it again" (John 12:28).

Four Divine Affirmations for Burdened Leaders

Paul also experienced divine affirmation on multiple occasions. I've found his encounter with Jesus while being held by Roman guards in Jerusalem to be especially powerful, although there is always some danger in exploring the life of Paul because of our tendency to supersize his walk with Jesus. We envision Paul casting out demons, performing miracles, and taking a break only to write more of the Bible. But that would be glossing over the many challenges he faced as a leader.

In Acts 23, Paul was in the middle of a difficult season. He had been run out of Ephesus by a riot, then traveled to Jerusalem with plans to travel to Rome. But while in Jerusalem, Paul was falsely accused of bringing a Greek convert into the temple. Zealous Jews started a riot and began to beat Paul. Roman soldiers saved him, but only because they believed he must be guilty of something. They arrested him. Paul had tried to reason with the rioters, but they interrupted his speech, shouting, "Rid the earth of him! He's not fit to live" (Acts 22:22)! By any standards of leadership, that's a bad day.

The next day Paul got a second opportunity to clear up the confusion by speaking to Jewish leaders at the Sanhedrin. But the situation went from bad to worse. "The dispute became so violent that the commander was afraid Paul would be torn to pieces by them" (Acts 23:10). Paul was taken from the Sanhedrin to the Roman barracks. If any leader needed affirmation, it was Paul.

"The following night the Lord stood near Paul and said, 'Take courage! As you have testified about me in Jerusalem, so you must also testify in Rome" (Acts 23:11).

This difficult passage in Paul's leadership journey provides four affirmations for every leader. When the burden gets heavy, take a page out of my dad's leadership playbook. Get alone in a place where you can connect with God and reflect on these powerful truths.

God Knows Where You Are
The following night, after the disaster before the Sanhedrin, "The Lord stood near Paul." Regardless of how alone or isolated you may feel, no matter how far off the beaten path of success, or out of the limelight you serve, God knows where you are.

There is a difference between the omnipresence of God and the presence of God. Knowing God is everywhere is not the same as God coming near. The following night, the Lord stood *near* Paul. He knows where you are, and he draws near.

God Knows What You Need
The first words Jesus spoke to Paul were, "Take courage!" Why? Because Jesus cared how Paul felt under the burden he was carrying and knew he desperately needed courage. Whenever Jesus saw hurting people, his first response was to be moved with compassion. His response is the same toward hurting leaders. Paul needed courage. You might need strength. Whatever the need, God knows.

God Remembers What You Have Done
Jesus told Paul, "As you have testified in Jerusalem"—a very interesting comment because Paul's time in Jerusalem was not very successful by any standard. In fact, the recurring reality of Paul's visits to Jerusalem after his conversion was that people there tried to kill him.

God cares about fruitfulness as well as faithfulness. But we must understand that he measures results differently. He leverages our obedience with those who have come before us and compounds our obedience with those who will come behind us. We look at our slice of the loaf, but God looks at the whole loaf. The question we must ask ourselves is: *Did I do my part?*

Five times in the letters to the seven churches of Revelation, Jesus says, as a point of commendation or encouragement, "I know your deeds." Others may not be paying much attention, but God remembers what you have done.

God Controls Where You Are Going
Jesus concluded his affirmation to Paul, saying, "So you must also testify in Rome." Paul had come to believe that part of his future ministry would play out in the city of Rome (Acts 19:21). God knew how important it would be for Paul to have the assurance that his life was not controlled by circumstances and that his future was safe in God's hand. Between Jerusalem and Rome, Paul would spend two years imprisoned in Caesarea, followed by the life-threatening encounters of a shipwreck and a snakebite. But Paul knew he was going to Rome. Your future is safe in God's hands too.

Just as much as Paul, God remembered where Jeroboam was, what he needed, what he'd done, and where he could have gone. Instead of becoming the benchmark for wicked kings, Jeroboam, could have ruled over a dynasty as enduring as king David's. Jeroboam's self-centered ambition provides a sobering lesson every leader needs to learn vicariously. Let nothing eclipse the God-given burden for the followers and the mission entrusted to you.

CHAPTER **06**

Worship

Worship

TRANSITIONAL
LEADERSHIP ERA

FOLLOWERS

Three
Hebrew leaders,
Shadrach, Meshach,
and Abednego

INFLUENCE

SITUATION

Three Hebrew
leaders in
Babylonian
captivity refuse
to worship
Nebuchadnezzar's
idol of gold

LEADER
King Nebuchadnezzar

> "O Nebuchadnezzar ... we will not serve your gods or worship the image of gold you have set up." —Daniel 3:16–18

Executive Summary

The ultimate prize for Satan is not damning a human spirit to eternal fire. It is robbing God of the worship he deserves from that human spirit, forever. There are three types of worship: false, vain, and true. True worship is a spiritual posture by which we affirm who God is and where he belongs in the hierarchy of our affections. Shadrach, Meshach, and Abednego modeled true worship, risking death over committing the sin of false worship that sent the Jews into exile. True worship in the life of a leader can produce amazing spiritual breakthroughs for followers.

I choose to place a high value on feedback. Ninety-eight percent of the time that choice serves me very well. But occasionally, feedback that should become white noise consumes way too much of my time. One such occasion taught me an unexpected lesson.

Part of my role as president of Missio Nexus included overseeing a national conference of Great Commission influencers from our network of churches, mission agencies, and educational institutions. By the time I transitioned out of that position, the conference attracted a thousand leaders who represented a diverse range of ages and theological perspectives within the evangelical tradition. They came from as many as thirty denominations and more than one hundred cross-denominational organizations.

Diversity of perspective is an asset for events like this in almost every way. But it worked against our desire to create unity through worship music. It was impossible to please more than sixty to seventy percent of the group. And the dissenters were always more vocal than everyone else.

After each conference, I went through a ritual of reviewing all the online evaluations submitted by attendees. One of the most common threads of negative feedback related to worship style. But since the worship would inevitably offend at least thirty percent of those in attendance, I didn't want that portion to be the next generation of mission leaders. I wanted to engage the upcoming generation, so the conference always pushed the envelope toward a more contemporary worship experience, at least as it related to the style of the band and the volume of the music.

One year an expression of negative feedback came outside the conference evaluation in the form of a letter sent by postal mail. One copy of the letter was sent to me and another to the chairman of our board, in two separate envelopes. The dissenter explained how deeply troubled he was by the worship music at the conference. He asserted that the guest worship leader had been on an ego trip, more concerned about bringing attention to himself than glory to God.

I was shocked to read this accusation. I had spent a significant amount of time with the worship leader and knew he is one of the most humble, godly, Scripture-grounded people I've ever met. He is a spiritual leader, who also happens to be an amazing musician and songwriter.

I decided to seek a conversation with the mission leader who sent the letter, so I asked my assistant to schedule a phone meeting. During the phone meeting, he explained his formula for evaluating the heart of a worship leader. He said if the lights in the auditorium are dim during worship, with spotlights on the worship leader, it's all about ego. You are watching someone who wants to be worshiped, not lead others in worship. I pushed back on his assertion of this bizarre formula to no avail. It became clear we would simply have to agree to disagree. I explained to the mission leader that he probably would not feel comfortable at our conference in future years, because the style of music wasn't going to change. He said he would never be back.

But then he was back. Not at our event; in my email inbox. During the next couple of months he sent me several links to blog posts and articles he claimed as reinforcement of his opinion. I confess I read one of them. It was a waste of my time. After receiving three or four more of his emails, I told him I wasn't reading them and asked him to please stop sending them. Then I just started hitting delete. A few months later, it was over.

The communication stopped, but my reflection on the exchange went deeper. There was an irony I didn't want to miss.

A Worship War Worth Fighting

I have come to believe the ultimate prize for Satan is not the satisfaction of damning a human spirit to eternal fire. It is robbing God of the worship he deserves from that human spirit, forever. There is a fundamental connection between worship and missions.

As John Piper explains: "Missions is not the ultimate goal of the church. Worship is. Missions exists because worship doesn't."[38] The spiritually lost state of humankind is important. The worthiness of God is preeminent.

Petty worship wars, like the disagreement I had with the mission leader, merely distract worshippers from the preeminent object of our affection. This distraction is a worship war worth fighting. But it's not about the style of songs, the volume of the music, or if the house lights are down when we sing.

In a passage widely understood to describe the motives of Satan in rebelling against God, Isaiah said:

> You said in your heart, "I will ascend to heaven; I will raise my throne above the stars of God; I will sit enthroned on the mount of assembly, on the utmost heights of the sacred mountain. I will ascend above the tops of the clouds; I will make myself like the Most High'" (Isa. 14:12–14).

Satan offered Jesus "the kingdoms of the world," saying, "If you worship me, it will all be yours" (Luke 4:7). Jesus responded: "It is written, 'Worship the Lord your God and serve him only'" (Luke 4:8). People are important to God as unique instruments of worship. God desires our worship for all eternity. He knows we experience the deepest sense of purpose and contentment when our lives are ordered around him. Again, to quote Piper, "God is most glorified in us, when we are most satisfied in him."[39]

Worship is central to mission. And mission is central to leadership. Leaders are pacesetters for followers. The most important trail that leaders blaze is marked by worship—by which we affirm who God is and where he belongs in the hierarchy of our affections.

King Nebuchadnezzar recognized the power of worship. He wanted first place in the hierarchy of his people's affections, so he created a golden opportunity to require everyone to bow to him. But he hadn't counted on the steadfast faith of Daniel's three Hebrew friends who resisted his command and braced for one of the most notable worship wars in the Bible.

Nebuchadnezzar's Head of Gold

The opening verses of Daniel 3 describe one of the most amazing leadership summits in the Bible. King Nebuchadnezzar summoned an impressive list of Babylonian leaders—"satraps, prefects, governors, advisors, treasurers, judges, magistrates and all the other provincial officials"—to come to the dedication of an image of gold he had set up (Dan. 3:2).

You don't need to know the difference between a satrap and a prefect to understand their significance here. The king of the most powerful empire of the ancient world at the time had decided that everybody who is anybody in leadership needed to be at this summit.

Nebuchadnezzar called this important leadership gathering to unveil an idol made of pure gold, standing ninety feet high and nine feet wide. Looking at this occasion in Daniel 3 in a broader context, we see an obvious connection with the dream revealed and explained in Daniel 2, where Daniel said:

> You looked, O king, and there before you stood a large statue—an enormous, dazzling statue, awesome in appearance. The head of the statue was made of pure gold, its chest and arms of silver, its belly and thighs of bronze, its legs of iron, its feet partly of iron and partly of baked clay (Dan. 2:31–33).

Daniel went on to explain that a rock struck the statue, first on the feet. Then the statue broke completely into pieces, becoming like chaff on a threshing floor, while the rock became a huge mountain and filled the whole earth. Daniel interpreted this dream to Nebuchadnezzar:

> You, O king, are the king of kings. The God of heaven has given you dominion and power and might and glory; in your hands he has placed mankind and the beasts of the field and the birds of the air. Wherever they live, he has made you ruler over them all. You are that head of gold (Dan. 2:37–38).

Nebuchadnezzar allowed Daniel to interpret the rest of the dream. But I think Nebuchadnezzar latched onto the phrase, "You are that head of gold"—the crowning glory of a large, enormous, dazzling, awesome-in-appearance statue.

Between Daniel 2 and 3, Nebuchadnezzar got busy. The leadership summit introduced in Daniel 3 is all about unveiling his large statue made of pure gold. The statue was a proxy for the king himself. Why be only the head of gold, when you can be the entire gold statue?

Worship is a central theme of this leadership interaction. The word *worship* is used ten times in thirty verses in Daniel 3. Worship of the image of gold was, by extension, worship of Nebuchadnezzar. No wonder he became "furious with rage" when he discovered three leaders at the summit—Shadrach, Meshach, and Abednego—who refused to bow to his idol. We can learn a lot from this familiar story, integrated with a big-picture perspective of worship in the Bible.

Three Types of Worship in the Bible

My study of the Bible suggests there are three types of worship: false, vain, and true. All three types occur in all four Leadership Eras of the Bible, and they continue today.

False worship begins with *deception* and results in *idolatry*. Satan deceives fallen humanity into believing a created, shiny object is worthy of worship in place of the Creator. But God said, "You shall have no other gods before me" (Ex. 20:3). Knowing the deception that accompanies the desire for a physical representation of divine power, God specifically prohibited making "an idol in the form of anything in heaven above or the earth beneath or in the waters below" (Ex. 20:4).

My experience leading mission teams and speaking to mission leaders in other countries has given me a firsthand opportunity to witness how deep the deception of idolatry can go. Demonic powers often reinforce the deception by manifesting in one way or another to people who worship idols, keeping them in bondage.

But idolatry is not limited to remote villages in far-away lands. A. W. Tozer said:

> Among the sins to which the human heart is prone, hardly any other is more hateful to God than idolatry, for idolatry is at bottom a libel on his character. The idolatrous heart assumes that God is other than he is—in itself a monstrous sin—and substitutes for the one true God one made after its own likeness.[40]

Vain worship begins with *pride* and results in *hypocrisy*. God despises vain worship just as much as false worship. God spoke through the prophet Amos to rebuke Israel with these strong words:

> I hate, I despise your religious feasts; I cannot stand your assemblies. Even though you bring me burnt offerings and grain offerings, I will not accept them. Though you bring me choice fellowship offerings, I will have no regard for them. Away with the noise of your songs! I will not listen to the music of your harps. But let justice roll on like a river, righteousness like a never-failing stream (Amos 5:21–24)!

Vain worship is more than a disconnect with God. It almost always makes onlookers feel unworthy of God. This could explain why Jesus gave some of his most powerful and pointed rebukes to vain worshipers. Speaking to the Pharisees, Jesus quoted the words of Isaiah:

> You hypocrites! Isaiah was right when he prophesied about you: "These people honor me with their lips, but their hearts are far from me. They worship me in vain; their teachings are but rules taught by men" (Matt. 15:7–9).

One of my favorite stories of D. L. Moody comes from his London evangelistic campaign in 1884. As the campaign meeting was getting started a local leader was invited to pray. The prayer droned on for what seemed like forever in a sanctimonious tone. Moody sensed the people getting restless. In a bold, unorthodox move, he stepped forward during the prayer and shouted, "Let us sing a hymn while our brother finishes his prayer."[41]

Moody didn't know that as he interrupted the prayer, a young medical student named Wilfred Grenfell was walking out of the building. Taken aback by Moody's act, Grenfell inquired as to the identity of such a brash leader on the platform. When he found out Moody was the speaker, Grenfell decided to stay, and by the end of the evening had devoted his life to Christ. Eventually Grenfell became a medical missionary to the people of Labrador, the northern region of Newfoundland in Canada. Moody's disruption of vain worship was as Christlike an action as the message he preached later that evening.

The Power of True Worship

True worship begins with *relationship* and results in *intimacy*. Jesus said to the Samaritan woman at the well:

> You Samaritans worship what you do not know; we worship what we do know, for salvation is from the Jews. Yet a time is coming and has now come when true worshipers will worship the Father in spirit and truth, for they are the kind of worshipers the Father seeks. God is spirit, and his worshipers must worship in spirit and truth (John 4:23–24).

Jesus emphasized the importance of worshiping in spirit and truth. Our spirit is the aspect of our being that enables us to have relationship with God. Paul said, "The Spirit himself testifies with our spirit that we are God's children" (Rom. 8:16). Truth is the means by which God reveals himself to us. Jesus said, "I am the way and the truth and the life. No one comes to the Father except through me" (John 14:6).

Among examples of true worship throughout the Bible, we find one of the most amazing in the National Leadership Era as Moses communed with God in the "tent of meeting." When the people saw Moses go into the tent, with the pillar of cloud at its entrance, "they all stood and worshiped, each at the entrance to his own tent" (Ex.

33:10). Inside the tent of meeting, "The LORD would speak to Moses face to face, as a man speaks with his friend" (Ex. 33:11).

I describe true worship as a spiritual posture by which we affirm who God is, and where he belongs in the hierarchy of our affections. The first responsibility of spiritual leaders is to lead followers into a relationship with God, fostering the kind of intimacy that flows from true worship.

Tozer said the most important thing about you is what comes to your mind when you think about God.[42] A right understanding of the nature and character of God is the gateway into an authentic, intimate relationship. Intimacy is not the same as familiarity, and it is not incompatible with awe. The combination of a reverential fear of God with mystery, fascination, admiration, and devotion "is the most enjoyable state and most purifying emotion the human soul can know."[43]

With this overview of three types of worship in the Bible, we can more fully appreciate how Shadrach, Meshach, and Abednego understood and expressed true worship.

True Worship as Spiritual Warfare

Shadrach, Meshach, and Abednego served as administrators over the province of Babylon. Daniel had requested their promotion after being placed in charge of all the wise men in Babylon. He served the king from the royal court in a special advisory role. Unlike his three Hebrew friends, it appears Daniel was exempted from the meeting where the king's image of gold was unveiled.[44]

The penalty for refusing to participate in worship of the image of gold had been announced in advance. Anyone who did not bow to it would be thrown into a burning hot furnace. Despite the capital cost of refusing to bow, the three Hebrew leaders understood that bowing to the image would be false worship. They also knew from experience that Nebuchadnezzar had a short fuse. His default leadership style combined threat and intimidation. Remember, Nebuchadnezzar had decided to execute all the wise men of Babylon for failing to tell him what he had dreamed, which in turn opened the door for Daniel and his friends to gain positions of influence.

Nebuchadnezzar's golden image gave physical representation to his oversized ego. When Daniel said, "You are that head of gold," the king only became more intoxicated with pride. I can imagine him lying awake at night envisioning his leadership summit with everyone who was anyone in his kingdom bowing down before the golden statue. Now three defiant Hebrews were rewriting the script. His honor was at stake.

Nebuchadnezzar offered Shadrach, Meshach, and Abednego one last chance to change their minds. In response they affirmed their refusal to participate in false worship:

> The God we serve is able to rescue us from it, and he will rescue us from your hand, O king. But even if he does not, we want you to know, O king, that we will not serve your gods or worship the image of gold you have set up (Dan. 3:17–18).

This is true worship in action. They affirmed God's power and his preeminent place in the hierarchy of their affections. They preferred death to disobedience. Every act of obedience takes new ground from the enemy and is therefore a form of spiritual warfare. Worship is the highest form of obedience. As Samuel reminded King Saul, obedience is better than sacrifice (1 Sam. 15:22).

The standoff between Nebuchadnezzar and the three Hebrew leaders became a high-profile and high-stakes power encounter in which God would demonstrate his preeminence not only over the king, but also over the people of Israel.

True Worship as a Key to Unlock Idolatry

It is important to remember the Jews were in captivity in Babylon because of false worship. They had refused to listen to the warning of the prophets and had prostituted themselves with idols. Jeremiah wept for his people, pleading for them to return to true worship.

God spoke through Jeremiah's lament: "I remember the devotion of your youth, how as a bride you loved me and followed me through the desert, through a land not sown" (Jer. 2:2). The prophet went on to say, "My people have exchanged their glory for worthless idols" (Jer. 2:11).

The irony of the leadership conversation between Nebuchadnezzar and the three Hebrew leaders is they would rather die than commit the very sin that sent the nation into exile in the first place. Upon being thrown into the furnace, their commitment to true worship was rewarded—when the pre-incarnate Christ met them in the flames.[45]

Peter is known for walking on water with Jesus. Shadrach, Meshach, and Abednego stood in fire with Jesus. In both cases, it was the presence of Jesus that made the difference.

Nebuchadnezzar already knew the God whom these three leaders worshiped. Daniel had told him about their God. It came as no surprise when the king called to the three in the furnace, "Servants of the Most High God, come out" (Dan. 3:26)! Upon seeing them unharmed, Nebuchadnezzar offered praise to their God and issued a decree warning the people of any nation or language who would say anything against this God.

God used this public act of true worship and leadership obedience to break the stronghold of idolatry over Israel. Ezekiel, a contemporary of Daniel, spoke about the captivity that resulted from Israel's idolatry:

> So I will put a stop to the lewdness and prostitution you began in Egypt. You will not look on these things with longing or remember Egypt anymore (Ezek. 24:27).

The power of obedience in the context of true worship cascaded across the nation of Israel. From that day forward, the people did not look at idols with longing hearts and did not live in bondage to the national sin of false worship. In the following years, the Jewish diaspora became renowned for their highly ethical, monotheistic faith in the true God. This fresh zeal for true worship took root even while they were away from their homeland and without the supportive structures of the priesthood or the sacrificial system.

One tangible expression of their liberation from idolatry was the synagogue system, which began during the later stages of the exile. Wherever ten Jewish families resided, they could form a synagogue for communal prayer and reading of Scripture. A nation of idol worshipers would have no appetite for a synagogue. But freed from the national bondage of false worship, synagogues became centers of Jewish spirituality, even attracting God-fearing Gentiles.

By the time Jesus came on the scene, the Jews would suffer from the legalism of the Pharisees, but not the polytheism of Canaan, Babylon, or their Greek and Roman conquers. Shadrach, Meshach, and Abednego's public standoff with Nebuchadnezzar became a key God used to unlock the chains of false worship for Israel. When the apostles wrestled with how to relate to Gentiles who were drawn to faith in Jesus, James affirmed, "Moses has been preached in every city from the earliest times and is read in the synagogues on every Sabbath" (Acts 15:21).

True Worship in Sacrifice, Music, and Leadership

Worship has become nearly synonymous with music for the church today, especially in North America. But that has not always been the case. In the Patriarchal Leadership Era, worship was most closely associated with sacrifice. To expose the hierarchy of Abraham's affections, God told him to offer his son Isaac as a sacrifice. Abraham went to the place for the sacrifice and told his servants: "Stay here with the donkey while I and the boy go over there. We will worship and then we will come back to you" (Gen. 22:5). When God directed Abraham to a ram caught in the bushes as a substitute for the sacrifice of Isaac, he revealed more of his divine character, "The LORD Will Provide." The entire worship experience revolved around the sacrifice.

In the National Leadership Era, worship was also associated with sacrifice. Moses told Pharaoh repeatedly to let the people of Israel go and worship the Lord. When Pharaoh told Moses to go along with the people, leaving only the flocks and herds behind, Moses refused. "Our livestock too must go with us ... We have to use some of them in worshiping the LORD our God" (Ex. 10:26).

After the transition from theocracy to monarchy in the National Leadership Era, worship became associated with both sacrifice and music. By the time King David had established his rule, he put gifted musicians "in charge of the music in the house of the LORD after the ark came to rest there" (1 Chron. 6:31). These men "ministered with music before the tabernacle, the Tent of Meeting, until Solomon built the temple of the LORD in Jerusalem" (1 Chron. 6:32).

The Transitional Leadership Era began when Nebuchadnezzar conquered Jerusalem, destroyed the temple, and took the Jews into exile in Babylon. When exile disrupted the sacrificial system, worship became less directly associated with sacrifice. The Jews felt deep pain and loss that made it harder to worship in song because they knew the temple had been destroyed.

But their music wasn't limited to the temple. Songs continued to provide an outlet for the spirit to express devotion to God. Psalm 137 reflects this tension:

> By the rivers of Babylon we sat and wept when we remembered Zion. There on the poplars we hung our harps, for there our captors asked us for songs, our tormentors demanded songs of joy; they said, "Sing us one of the songs of Zion!"

> How can we sing the songs of the LORD while in a foreign land? If I forget you, O Jerusalem, may my right hand forget its skill. May my tongue cling to the

roof of my mouth if I do not remember you, if I do
not consider Jerusalem my highest joy (Ps. 137:1–6).

Even pagan leaders like Nebuchadnezzar associated music with
worship. The signal to bow to the statue of gold was the "sound of
the horn, flute, lyre, harp, and all kinds of music" (Dan. 3:7).

By the close of the Transitional Leadership Era the temple was
rebuilt and the system of sacrifices reinstated.

During the Spiritual Leadership Era, with the ministry of Jesus
and the early Church, worship became reconnected to sacrifice in
the temple. Although the absence of the monarchy appears to have
diminished the role of musicians when compared to the apex of David's
rule, music retained a meaningful place in the Christian community.
Jesus and his disciples sang a hymn after celebrating the Passover, which
included the sacrifice of a lamb (Mark 14:26). Paul and Silas prayed and
sang hymns to God in a midnight worship experience, while sacrificing
for their faith in prison (Acts 16:25).

Paul reconnected worship with sacrifice in the church sub-phase of
the Spiritual Leadership Era by exhorting believers: "Offer your bodies
as living sacrifices, holy and pleasing to God—this is your spiritual act
of worship" (Rom. 12:1). He instructed the church in Ephesus:

> Speak to one another with psalms, hymns and
> spiritual songs. Sing and make music in your heart
> to the Lord, always giving thanks to God the Father
> for everything, in the name of our Lord Jesus Christ
> (Eph. 5:19–20).

Music is a powerful, emotive, and creative force that connects
the will with the emotions. But when the understanding of worship
is limited to music, leaders who are not musically inclined will too
often delegate the music and with it, the worship. It is wise for leaders
to delegate music to musicians. It is wrong for leaders to delegate
worship to anyone. Worship is a leadership function. Perhaps no
leader in the Bible modeled this more powerfully than Moses.

The Presence Principle

True worship is built on relationship and results in intimacy. From
this spiritual posture we affirm who God is, and we ensure his
rightful place in the hierarchy of our affections. Effective spiritual
leaders view true worship as a priority leadership function.

The greatest gift leaders can offer their followers is a life lived in the overflow of intimacy with God. This is an essential and foundational building block of spiritual authority, giving evidence to the powerful presence of God in the life and ministry of the leader.[46]

When leaders make true worship a priority, they can usher in spiritual breakthroughs for followers beyond anything imaginable. Yet leaders are too often lured by leadership or ministry fads, chasing the latest shiny object. A. W. Tozer said:

> I cannot speak for you, but I want to be among those who worship. I do not want just to be a part of some great ecclesiastical machine where the pastor turns the crank and the machine runs.[47]

Moses understood that success without the presence of God is failure. When offered an angelic escort into the Promised Land, but without the presence of God, Moses responded:

> If your Presence does not go with us, do not send us up from here. How will anyone know that you are pleased with me and your people unless you go with us (Ex. 33:15–16)?

God responded to Moses: "I will do the very thing you have asked, because I am pleased with you and I know you by name" (Ex. 33:17). This is a powerful description of true worship, based on relationship, resulting in intimacy. But beyond an awareness of God's presence, true worship builds on an understanding of God's character. Moses, longing for a deeper revelation of the nature of God, appealed to him, "Now show me your glory" (Ex. 33:18).

God instructed Moses to stand in the cleft of a rock, which he covered with his hand while passing by. God then gave Moses the most comprehensive revelation of his nature recorded in Scripture:

> The LORD, the LORD, the compassionate and gracious God, slow to anger, abounding in love and faithfulness, maintaining love to thousands, and forgiving wickedness, rebellion and sin. Yet he does not leave the guilty unpunished (Ex. 34:6–7a).

Moses was alone on the mountain when God revealed himself in these words. But this description of God's character became imprinted in the memory of the nation of Israel. David referenced Moses's experience with God in Psalm 103:

He made his ways known to Moses, his deeds to the people
of Israel: The LORD is compassionate and gracious, slow
to anger and abounding in love (Ps. 103:7–8).

The Inseparable Relationship of Worship and Missions

This chapter began with an assertion that worship is at the heart of
missions, and missions is central to leadership. True worship puts
God, not people, at the center of mission. It doesn't deny the reality
of hell or the spiritually lost state of humankind. But it does give
priority to the worthiness of God, who deserves to be worshiped
forever by all his creation.

A people-centered theology of missions makes us vulnerable
to allowing prejudice and bias to disrupt our engagement in God's
redemptive work, especially among people who would do us harm. The
evil deeds of terrorists call for judgment, not mercy. But regardless,
when lost people die, God is eternally robbed of their worship.

This is the story of the prophet Jonah. God called him to preach
repentance to the wicked people of Nineveh. But Jonah hated the
Ninevites and believed God should judge them. He wanted them to
be punished more than he wanted God to be worshiped—the danger
of a people-centered theology of missions that is not balanced by
a God-centered perspective of true worship. It is easy to believe
those who have perpetrated horrific evil acts are more deserving of
punishment than God is of worship.

Jonah realized his people-centered focus on judgment was out
of sync with the character of God. Jonah experienced not joy, not
worship, but rather displeasure and depression after the people
of the great city of Nineveh did just what he told them to do. They
repented, and God relented. By any definition of ministry this was
success. But not for Jonah.

His prayer to God reveals why he didn't want to go to Nineveh in
the first place. And it was rooted in his understanding of the nature
of God, based on the revelation to Moses.

O LORD, is this not what I said when I was still at
home? That is why I was so quick to flee to Tarshish.
I knew that you are a gracious and compassionate
God, slow to anger and abounding in love, a God
who relents from sending calamity" (Jonah 4:2).

Jonah is saying: *God, you are so predictable. I know what you are like, and I knew you would rather forgive than condemn. But I hate the Ninevites and wanted them to be punished.* Jonah had developed a human-centered understanding of mission and was focused on his hatred for the Ninevites. But true worship stems from a God-centered theology of missions that draws our attention to his worthiness to be praised by all of creation for all of eternity.

By his very nature, God is on mission. True worship is both the goal and the fuel of missions, and is therefore central to Christian leadership. When we understand who God is, and give him the rightful place in our lives, we can't help but join him. And that's the leadership legacy of Shadrach, Meshach, and Abednego.

CHAPTER 07

Risk

Risk

TRANSITIONAL
LEADERSHIP ERA

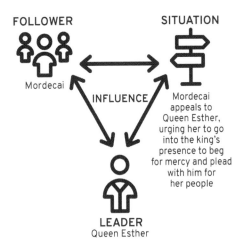

FOLLOWER

Mordecai

INFLUENCE

SITUATION

Mordecai appeals to Queen Esther, urging her to go into the king's presence to beg for mercy and plead with him for her people

LEADER
Queen Esther

"I and my maids will fast as you do. When this is done, I will go to the king, even though it is against the law. And if I perish, I perish."
—Esther 4:16

Executive Summary

A leader's greatest opportunity for impact will almost always require the biggest sacrifice and greatest risk. There is no spiritual merit associated with increasing risk by failing to plan. Nothing about planning is incompatible with prayer. Unbiblical teaching on the character of God, suffering, and risk, has swept the North American church. Queen Esther's story is most often referenced for the importance of timing and opportunity, with the words of Mordecai, "for such a time as this." We can only make sense of these five words by remembering the five words of Esther, "If I perish, I perish."

"What did you think was going to happen?"

This wasn't the response we were expecting. It came from a seasoned cross-cultural worker in a Muslim country where I had been serving along with five others on a summer mission team. After having been arrested in another city, we had just arrived back in the world-class city where the worker was based.

I was a twenty-three-year-old college student at the time, but I remember the experience vividly. I still have the journal I kept that summer. It sits on my desk, right by my phone, open to a page where I made promises to God about my future. I want to remind myself of those promises every morning when I start my day.

As a team, our mission was to sell Bibles, as well as other books about life—based on the teachings of Jesus. We went from store to store in major cities. All the material had been printed locally, and though we had been advised that distributing it freely would be problematic, it was perfectly legal to sell. At least that's what we thought. We memorized some phrases in the local language and took to the streets.[48]

One of our team members got arrested within the first two weeks. When he didn't return one evening, we moved to a different place in the city, in the middle of the night. We were surprised when he reconnected with us a few days later. He had quite a story to tell, along with a case of lice from the jail where he was held.

Local officials had taken him to a train station to send him out of the country. But when his escorts weren't looking, he escaped. It sounds a lot more like a spiritual James Bond movie than it really was. Perhaps because of the lice.

He had to lay low for a few days before we all relocated to another city to start over. After almost two weeks of fruitful book selling, we were looking forward to a few days of rest and relaxation. The plan was to meet at a park, load up our van, and head out of town. What we didn't know was our team leader had been arrested earlier in the day. The police had confiscated the van and all our supplies. We wouldn't be going anywhere near R & R.

We waited at our rendezvous point in the park until two plain-clothes police officers came and found us. That evening we were reunited with our leader in a holding station with about ten to fifteen other people. To say we stood out among the locals—Palestinians and Egyptians—would be an understatement.

The guards kept the lights on twenty-four hours a day in the holding area, so it was hard to sleep. Not to mention the park benches pushed together to form a bed. Some of the benches had old, broken-down cardboard boxes on them as makeshift mattresses. I used my shoes for a pillow.

We passed the time by playing games. Hockey can be played with three coins on the top of a desk. American football was possible with a piece of paper folded into a small triangle and pushed along with your finger. The games were a big hit with our cellmates and somewhat baffling to the guards. And it totally changed the atmosphere in the holding cell. But it didn't address the bigger question we were asking, "What happens next?"

After three days, we were brought before a judge. He said there wasn't enough information to make a ruling on our case and sent us to a hostel under house arrest. The police kept our van, our passports, and our supplies. We were more comfortable in the hostel than the holding cell, but we were still in limbo. Eventually we decided to wander away from the hostel on foot to see how much freedom of movement they would allow.

We found ourselves standing outside the US Embassy, trying to decide if we should ask for help, when a young man from that city walked up to us and began talking in perfect English. He asked what we were doing. We decided there wasn't a lot of risk in telling him the truth.

He said, "My father was a judge, and then became a senator." Our hopes were soaring until he added, "He's dead, but I still think I can help you."

We told him where we were staying and welcomed anything he could do to help. Within two days this teenager, who was headed to the US on a soccer scholarship, called our hostel and said, "It's all worked out. You are free to go."

We told him that was awesome but until the police gave back our van, passports and supplies, we weren't going anywhere.

He said, "Oh, sure. They'll bring those back soon."

Within an hour we had everything that had been taken from us, and we were instructed to leave the city. Our new Muslim friend arrived as we were packing. He insisted on hosting us for dinner at his house before we went on our way. Then after dinner, he convinced us to stay the night. Middle Eastern hospitality *is* all it's cracked up to be.

The following day we drove back to the city where the cross-cultural worker was located. We told him our story. We assumed our summer experience was over and we would need to go home. It was just too risky to start over in another city.

That's when he responded, "What did you think was going to happen?"

After a pep talk, he got out a map and began exploring options for where we should go next. Our team adventure continued in another city, including another arrest. The judge there sentenced us to three months in jail, to be suspended if we left the country. That's when the trip was formally over.

That summer of faith-stretching adventure ruined my life for ordinary Christianity. Looking back, I realize we were never in real physical danger. And the organization that planned our trip acted responsibly. But the experience opened a window for me. I caught a clearer glimpse than ever before of the risks many others take for the sake of the gospel.

The opportunity to make a significant impact almost always comes with significant risk. In fact, the two are directly related. A leader's greatest opportunity for impact will almost always require the biggest sacrifice and greatest risk. That's why the story of Queen Esther is most often referenced for the importance of timing and opportunity, with the words of Mordecai, for "such a time as this."

We can only make sense of these five words by remembering the five words of Esther, "If I perish, I perish." One of my earliest leadership mentors taught me a one-word definition of leadership: Risk. It comes with the territory. Esther understood this. Her story inspires us. And yet why do we work so hard to take the risk out of following Jesus today?

When God Is Too Safe

The C. S. Lewis book, *The Lion, the Witch, and the Wardrobe,* recounts the adventures of four children in the magical kingdom of Narnia. At the center of the allegory is Aslan, the Christ-figure in the story. Readers learn Aslan's identity in a classic exchange between the children and Mr. and Mrs. Beaver:

"Is he a man?" asked Lucy.

"Aslan a man!" said Mr. Beaver sternly. "Certainly not. I tell you he is King of the wood and the son of the great emperor-beyond-the-sea. Don't you know who is King of the Beasts? Aslan is a lion—*the* Lion, the great Lion."

"Ooh!" said Susan. "I'd thought he was a man. Is he—quite safe? I shall feel rather nervous about meeting a lion."

"That you will, dearie, and no mistake" said Mrs. Beaver; "if ever there's anyone who can appear before Aslan without their knees knocking, they're either braver than most or else just silly."

"Then he isn't safe?" said Lucy.

"Safe?" said Mr. Beaver; "don't you hear what Mrs. Beaver tells you? Who said anything about safe? 'Course he isn't safe. But he's good. He's the king, I tell you."[49]

Christianity, particularly in the West, has venerated safety. In doing so, we have committed libel against the character of God, remaking him in our own image. God isn't safe. To perpetuate this unbiblical understanding of God we must reinterpret much of the Bible and completely ignore the teachings of Jesus.

A. W. Tozer described this false-worship reimagining of God:

> The God of the modern evangelical rarely astonishes anybody. He manages to stay pretty much within the constitution. Never breaks over our bylaws. He's a very well behaved God and very denominational and very much one of us, and we ask Him to help us when we're in trouble and look to Him to watch over us when we're asleep. The God of the modern evangelical isn't a God I could have much respect for. But when the Holy Spirit shows us God as he is we admire Him to the point of wonder and delight.[50]

Unbiblical teaching on the character of God, suffering, and risk has swept the North American church like an urban legend on Facebook. It is accepted and shared without a second thought. It's fake theology, which is worse than fake news. At the core of this teaching is the idea that God loves us so much he would never ask us to do anything that is difficult or dangerous—certainly not something that could cost us our lives. To accept this fake theology requires some mental gymnastics as you read the Bible. Psychologists refer to this mental state as cognitive dissonance, in which thoughts, beliefs, or attitudes are inconsistent with behavioral decisions.

But the biblical perspective of risk is unequivocal. Consider how John Piper describes the teaching of Jesus on risk:

> By removing eternal risk, Christ calls his people to continual temporal risk.

With staggering promises of everlasting joy, Jesus unleashed a movement of radical, loving risk-takers. "You will be delivered up even by parents ... and some of you they will put to death" (Luke 21:16). Only some. Which means it might be you and it might not. That's what risk means. It is not risky to shoot yourself in the head. The outcome is certain. It is risky to serve Christ in a war zone. You might get shot. You might not.

Christ calls us to take risks for kingdom purposes. Almost every message of American consumerism says the opposite: Maximize comfort and security—now, not in heaven. Christ does not join that chorus. To every timid saint, wavering on the edge of some dangerous gospel venture, he says, "Fear not, you can only be killed" (Luke 12:4). Yes, by all means maximize your joy! How? For the sake of love, risk being reviled and persecuted and lied about, "for your reward is great in heaven" (Matt. 5:11–12).[51]

Celebrating Sacrifice—Conditionally

Jesus-followers in the West celebrate examples of suffering, sacrifice, and redemptive risk in the lives of others when we are separated from them by time and distance. We love historical risk-takers in the Bible and the saga of Church history. We love contemporary risk-takers if they live on a faraway continent. Separated from these heroes of faith by history or geography, we feel insulated from the expectation we should follow their lead, risking comfort and safety for the gospel.

This allows us to read their biographies and include their stories in our teaching. But when God raises up risk-taking radicals in our time and our town, we are confronted with a dilemma. To affirm they are living a "normal" Christian life shines the spotlight brightly on our own complacency. The alternative is to label them fanatics, believing they are going too far, because God would never ask normal people to embrace this level of risk. And yet we don't label soldiers as fanatics when they engage in active, risky military service; on the contrary, we hold their patriotism and sacrifice in high esteem.

I realize you might think I'm being too hard on the North American church. Or that I'm engaging in hyperbole to make my point. But I'm not. For years I've heard sincere Jesus-followers explain why we can't send workers to the people around the world who most need the gospel. The mission is just too dangerous.

I led the largest network of Great Commission-oriented leaders in North America for nine years. The line of people at mission agency doors willing to go to the hard places is not empty, but it is short. To return to the words of John Piper, "It is not risky to shoot yourself in the head. The outcome is certain. It is risky to serve Christ in a war zone. You might get shot. You might not." Some have gone to war zones for Jesus and were martyred. I understand why parents are reluctant to release their children into a war zone. But there's more to this story.

In recent years some of the most unreached peoples, in some of the most dangerous and least accessible places, have been displaced by terrorism and civil war. Their displacement has fueled global migration on an unprecedented scale. As a result, many of the same people in high-risk countries with little or no access to the gospel are now living in refugee camps. They are hoping against hope for the chance of winning the refugee lottery so they can start over among us.

Problem solved. Or not.

Some of the loudest voices in the United States against refugee resettlement are Jesus-followers. The core of their message is a desire to keep our country safe. Welcoming refugees, they believe, is just too risky. The facts actually show the chances of being killed by a refugee in the United States are 1 in 3.64 billion. It's comparable to the risk of dying from falling out of bed. So welcoming strangers is not a significant risk at all. Safety and compassion are not mutually exclusive.

Going where the refugees live is too dangerous, many say. Now, in God's providence, these unreached people are desperate to come to us. But again, many say we can't let that happen. It just wouldn't be safe.

I've tried to imagine how we could explain our risk-averse behavior to God. Maybe the animals will be able to talk in heaven. And Mr. Beaver will say, "Who said anything about safe? 'Course he isn't safe. But he's good. He's the king, I tell you."

Esther's Unlikely Rise to Royalty

Esther fits into the Transitional Leadership Era of the Bible. The backstory of her rise to influence began with King Xerxes hosting a banquet in the citadel of Susa, in modern-day Iran. The king invited his nobles, officials, military leaders, princes, and provincial leaders. Queen Vashti also hosted a banquet for the noble women at the king's palace.

On the seventh day of the king's banquet—remember, Middle Eastern hospitality is legendary—Xerxes was drunk and decided to parade Queen Vashti in front of his honored guests. The king sent seven eunuchs to bring Vashti to his banquet, but it appears that she resented the king's objectification of her beauty and refused to come. Vashti's refusal caused King Xerxes to lose face in a most public setting. He became angry and consulted with seven nobles, the highest in his kingdom, about what to do. They determined Vashti should be made an example; she would be banished, and her royal position would be given to someone else. The beauty contest to find a new queen produced an unlikely addition to the royal palace: a Jewish young woman named Esther. In unforeseen circumstances, she was ushered into a place of leadership and influence by the providence of God.

The subplot of Esther is the tension between her uncle Mordecai, and Haman, a nobleman promoted by the king to a "seat of honor higher than that of all the other nobles" (Es. 3:1). Mordecai refused to kneel down and pay honor to Haman as all the other royal officials did.

Notice the echoes from the previous chapter's leadership interactions involving Nebuchadnezzar and Daniel and his three Hebrew friends: a big gathering of the top officials in the land, a king's bruised ego and accompanying consequences, a demand to bow down, and a righteous refusal to bow. The hierarchy of a person's affections sometimes requires engaging in risky situations. Risk is a test of true devotion.

When Haman learned of Mordecai's refusal to bow, he had no choice but to show his power. Haman became obsessed with putting Mordecai to death. And when Haman learned Mordecai was a Jew, he determined that simply killing one defiant man wasn't enough. He began plotting and scheming "for a way to destroy all Mordecai's people, the Jews, throughout the whole kingdom of Xerxes" (Es. 3:6).

Haman eventually spoke to King Xerxes about a "certain people" in the kingdom with different customs and made a case for why it was "not in the king's best interest to tolerate them" (Es. 3:8). Haman was so intent on convincing the king of his plan he offered to contribute the funds needed to carry out the plan.

Xerxes signed off on the plan, told Haman to keep his money, and gave him the signet ring—a symbol of royal power. Once Haman's plan was in place, Mordecai heard about it and showed his displeasure by tearing his clothes, putting on sackcloth and ashes, and going about wailing loudly and bitterly.

Esther Risks All

When word reached Esther that her uncle was publicly distressed, she was deeply concerned for him. She sent her attendants to find out what was troubling him. Mordecai explained Haman's plan to Hathach, the eunuch sent by Esther, and passed along a copy of the edict for the annihilation of the Jews.

Mordecai told Hathach to urge Esther to "go into the king's presence to beg for mercy and plead with him for her people" (Es. 4:8). But Esther sent the eunuch back to Mordecai to explain that it was against the law to approach the king without being summoned—and punishable by death. She also explained it had been thirty days since the king had requested to see her.

In turn, Mordecai sent a message back to Esther, reminding her of God's sovereignty and highlighting the unique opportunity before her, "for such a time as this." She responded with the clear understanding of the risk and replied, "If I perish, I perish."

The irony of this story is unmistakable. Vashti was banished for refusing to appear before the king when summoned. But Esther's opportunity hinged on taking the risk to appear before the king without being summoned. Everything was on the line.

Why Opportunity Requires Risk

Esther's story reminds us that opportunity and risk go together. You can't have one without the other. And the greater the opportunity, the bigger the risk. The opportunity for your greatest impact is likely to come at a point in your journey when you have the most to lose. Younger leaders are often less risk averse. They have less to lose and more time to recover if they do lose. Risk becomes harder when influence becomes greater. With more experience, leaders also have more concern for their reputation. They worry about finding what's next if they fail.

It is tempting for emerging leaders to look at others who have "made it" and wonder why they are so cautious. Conversely, seasoned leaders look at younger leaders and think: *Talk to me in fifteen years.*

One of the challenges of leadership is learning how to blend the wisdom and experience of maturity with the risk-taking zeal of youth. When you add wisdom to zeal it doesn't have to water down the zeal. Wisdom softens the rough edges of zeal, making it less presumptuous and more humble. Zeal is not diluted by wisdom, but by unbelief.

During my mission team's misadventures, I found myself paralyzed by fear after my teammate got arrested. I approached a store and thought to myself, *If I go in there to sell my books someone is going to get angry and I'm going to get arrested.* I reasoned it to be too risky.

As I faced my fear, God met me in this passage from Hebrews:

> So do not throw away your confidence; it will be
> richly rewarded. You need to persevere so when
> you have done the will of God, you will receive
> what was promised. For in just a little while, 'He
> who is coming will come and will not delay. But my
> righteous one will live by faith. And if he shrinks
> back, I will not be pleased with him.' But we are not
> of those who shrink back and are destroyed, but of
> those who believe and are saved (Heb. 10:35–39).

The Mutual Benefits of Prayer and Planning

What I love about Esther's response to Mordecai is her instinct for serious prayer, which the Jews always associated with fasting. She asked Mordecai to leverage his influence in Susa to mobilize prayer and fasting. It appears Esther's faith had influenced her attendants as they also joined in the three days of prayer and fasting.

Then she committed to action: "When this is done, I will go to the king, even though it is against the law. And if I perish, I perish" (Es. 4:16).

Esther emerged from prayer and fasting with a plan. She didn't just get up from her prayer closet and march into the king's inner court to ask for mercy. Esther put on her royal robes and stood in the inner court of the palace where she knew the king could see her from his throne. Her heart must have pounded for the brief moment between the time the king saw her and when he raised his gold scepter, signaling approval for her to approach.

Even then Esther did not raise the issue of Haman's plot to destroy the Jews. She asked the king to bring Haman as a special guest to a banquet she had prepared for them. At the banquet, when the king asked what Esther wanted—up to half the kingdom—she asked them to attend another banquet the following day, where she would answer the king's request.

When did Esther develop this plan? It clearly didn't pop into her mind while she was waiting for the king to lift his golden scepter, because she had already prepared the first banquet. Esther designed a masterful plan during the three days of prayer and fasting. At some point in her prayerful planning, ideas began to emerge. She no doubt talked them over with the eunuchs who attended her and worked closely with the king.

There is no spiritual merit associated with increasing risk by failing to plan. Nothing about planning is incompatible with prayer. These two responsibilities of leadership are not mutually exclusive. One of the reasons I'm so deeply connected with 12Stone Church in my home city of Atlanta is the culture of serious prayer that seamlessly integrates with strategic planning. This combination fuels vision-driven risk, even when there is much to lose.

My friend Kevin Myers founded 12Stone Church and serves as senior pastor. He sets the tone for our congregation by elevating prayer as our highest value. I've been part of 12Stone since 2006 and have watched it grow from about 3,500 people in one location to nearly 20,000 people in eight locations. No doubt many have come from other churches, but even so, I've seen more people baptized at 12Stone than all the rest of my ministry combined, including my many trips abroad.

At the peak of 12Stone's growth, when the mother church had established three additional campuses, God spoke to Kevin about a five-campus simultaneous launch to help us reach more people in our county for Jesus. My first thought when I heard this vision was: *Who does this? One campus, sure. Two, maybe. But five campuses, simultaneously? Really? Why take such a massive risk when you have arrived and have so much to lose if it doesn't work?*

The big answer to my questions was clear. Kevin understood the five-campus launch to be an unmistakable God-prompt. He recognized how a leader's greatest opportunities for impact are married to the biggest risks. That's why every leader must undergird opportunities and risks with prayer and careful planning.

My wife and I experienced the excitement of helping launch one of the original satellite campuses so we knew right away we would be part of the launch team for the new five-campus vision. And we are amazed at how God blessed this high-risk venture that combined serious prayer and strategic planning. Being part of something like this creates a spiritual adrenaline rush for which there is no substitute.

The Consequences of Risk-Averse Discipleship

In Luke 19 Jesus told a story about a man of noble birth who went away to be made king and had plans to return. He called ten of his servants and gave each of them a *mina*, which was worth about three month's wages. The nobleman told his servants to "put this money to work until I come back" (Luke 19:13). When he returned as king, he sent for the servants to find out what they had accomplished with his money.

One of the servants generated a tenfold increase on the king's money. This servant was commended and given responsibility for ten cities. Another of the servants earned five additional minas. He was also commended and given charge over five cities.

A third servant came to the king saying, "Sir, here is your mina; I have kept it laid away in a piece of cloth" (Luke 19:20). The king rebuked this servant, asking, "Why didn't you put my money on deposit, so that when I came back, I could have at least collected the interest" (Luke 19:23)?

What can we learn about risk from this story? The servants had to take a risk in order to gain a reward, and the greater the risk, the greater the reward. You don't get a tenfold increase by putting money in the bank. The man who played it safe was rebuked. His mina was taken and given to the man who had earned ten by taking a greater risk. When this decision was questioned in the story, the king said: "I tell you that everyone who has, more will be given, but as for the one who has nothing, even what he has will be taken away" (Luke 19:26).

If a person has nothing, how can you take "even what he has" away? The mina in the story represents the giftedness and opportunities God gives us to advance his kingdom. We don't get to determine what or how much he endows, only whether we will use it all and use it well. The investment is his—the risk is ours. Ultimately, he will measure our return on risk.

Sadly, most Jesus-followers don't even know their strengths and spiritual gifts. Failure to discover and develop what God has placed within us is like wrapping our giftedness in a cloth and burying it in the ground. The king will not reward this risk-averse behavior. Leaders who don't help followers put their mina to work for the king are perpetuating an unbiblical expression of risk-averse discipleship.

If we imagine the mina as seeds given to plant a crop, the king would say to the servant who wrapped them in a cloth: *I wasn't asking you to protect the seeds. I wanted you to produce fruit. Since you have no fruit, I'm taking the seeds you have and giving them to the one who harvested a crop.*

The Cost of Too Much Love

One of my favorite missionary heroes is C. T. Studd. In 1885 he turned his back on a life of privilege in England to serve as a missionary in China—as part of Hudson Taylor's China Inland Mission (today OMF International). Studd later served in India, then returned to England in midlife because of chronic health issues. People described him as a "museum of diseases."

C. T. Studd was also a quote machine. He would have attracted quite a following on Twitter. Entire booklets have been printed of his quotes, and tens of thousands of social media posts repeat his words to this day. One of my all-time favorites is, "Some wish to live within the sound of church or chapel bell, I want to run a rescue shop within a yard of hell." His life story is one chapter of kingdom risk after another.

Through a bizarre turn of events, C. T. felt God calling him to leave England again in 1910 to go to the heart of Africa in one final risk of faith. If you want the whole story, read Norman Grubb's biography, *C. T. Studd Cricketer & Pioneer*. By this time C. T. was fifty years old. But age and illness had not changed his attitude, as he revealed in this quote: "Men can save their fellows from an angry sea or a house on fire only at great personal risk."

Studd presented the challenge of pioneer work in Africa to a group of business leaders who agreed to support the venture on one condition—he would need to get the green light from a doctor. The report came back from the doctor—a red light. The business leaders put severe limits on how far into the heart of Africa C. T. could go, but he refused to accept those limits. Support for the project was withdrawn.

C. T. wrote of his business leader friends, "Too much love is sometimes as bad as too much hate." They loved him too much to allow him to risk his life for the gospel. He responded to them: "God has called me to go, and I will go. I will blaze the trail, though my grave may only become a stepping stone that younger men may follow."[52]

C. T. died in the heart of Africa, twenty years later, after founding a new mission, known today as WEC International.

A risk-averse version of following Jesus is easily passed on to the next generation as leaders, parents, and others in authority withhold support for spiritual ventures and create obstacles that deter bold action. A few in every generation, like C. T. Studd, will not be denied the opportunity. Yet many gospel-motivated risk-takers who set aside daring ambitions will be cheered by people around them with too much love.

The dilemma of the risk-taker is not new. Paul experienced it while visiting Philip the evangelist on route to Jerusalem, when a prophet named Agabus came from Judea to visit.

[Agabus] took Paul's belt and tied his own hands and feet with it and said, the Holy Spirit says, "In this way the Jews of Jerusalem will bind the owner of this belt and will hand him over to the Gentiles" (Acts 21:11).

Agabus didn't say Paul shouldn't go. He simply prophesied about the difficulties Paul would experience along the way. When Paul's friends and colleagues heard this warning, they pleaded with Paul not to go up to Jerusalem. I think we can all understand why. If something like this happened today, we also would assume God was warning a person of coming danger so it could be avoided.

But that's not how Paul understood this message. He answered his friends:

> Why are you weeping and breaking my heart? I am ready not only to be bound, but also to die in Jerusalem for the name of the Lord Jesus (Acts 21:13).

Paul isn't quoting Esther, but he is reaffirming her commitment to seize God-directed opportunities in the face of great risk. "If I perish, I perish."

CHAPTER 08

Humility

Humility

SPIRITUAL
LEADERSHIP ERA

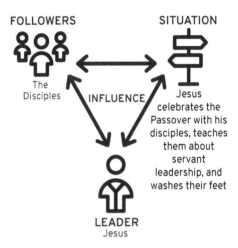

FOLLOWERS

The
Disciples

INFLUENCE

SITUATION

Jesus
celebrates the
Passover with his
disciples, teaches
them about
servant
leadership, and
washes their feet

LEADER
Jesus

"The kings of the Gentiles lord it over them; and those who exercise
authority over them call themselves Benefactors. But you are not to
be like that." —Luke 22:25–26

"Now that I, your Lord and Teacher, have washed your feet, you
also should wash one another's feet. I have set you an example that
you should do as I have done for you." —John 13:14–15

Executive Summary

Pride hides from the consciousness of leaders behind a mask of
overconfidence. Overconfidence isn't just annoying to followers. It is
dangerous for leaders. Overconfidence amplifies the temptation to fall in
love with our ideas and become rigid in our perspective. Overconfidence
whispers into an echo chamber of subconscious thought, *You're really
smart, really good at what you do, and almost always right.* The universal
antidote for hubris is humility. Never has there been a more powerful role
model of leadership humility than Jesus. The leadership mindset of Jesus
informs how we relate to status, service, sacrifice, and success.

I saw an either-or question on social media that piqued my curiosity: Would you rather be able to speak every language or play every instrument? It got me thinking about other either-or questions. For instance, would you rather be the wisest person in the world or the humblest person in the world? To ask it another way, would you want to be like Solomon or Moses?

Most Jesus-followers associate wisdom with Solomon. We less often connect humility with Moses. Yet we find this parenthetical statement in Numbers 12:3, "(Now Moses was a very humble man, more humble than anyone on the face of the earth.)"

When I was a student in Bible college one of my classmates asked the professor about this verse. My classmate said, "Assuming Moses wrote the Pentateuch, wouldn't it be prideful to say you are the most humble person on the earth?" The professor pointed out that the verse appears in parentheses because scholars assume an editor added it.

I find it easier to admit my lack of patience than my lack of humility. There is something about pride that wants to hide in the dark corners of my heart, perhaps because exposing it is the first step to expelling it. I learned a lesson in humility in an unusual way during the short-term mission trip I described in the previous chapter.

When our team was in the holding cell, after being arrested, one of the guards singled me out to come with him. I had no idea what to expect and no way to ask since he didn't speak English. He took me to the bathroom and gave me a push broom, a rag, and a garbage bag. Then he motioned for me to clean the place up. The floor was covered with standing water because pockets of trash were blocking the drains in the floor. The sinks were disgusting with dark hairs clinging to the basin like tiny insects holding on for dear life. The toilets were the squat variety and, well, I'll spare you any further details.

As I got started cleaning, the guard left me alone. Soon I discovered my feelings about this assignment were changing. It wasn't only the filthiness of the job that repulsed me, it was also the sense of humiliation. My mental pushback wasn't primarily about germs, it was about pride. And with my pride exposed, the Holy Spirit began to speak to me. I reflected on Jesus, who left the splendor and majesty of heaven to take on human likeness, to be born in a barn.

My perspective on the incarnation changed, as did my attitude about my cleaning assignment. The Holy Spirit said, "You came to this country because you wanted to tell people about Jesus. What if I'm giving you an opportunity to witness to this guard?" I decided to throw myself into my work with the goal of making the bathroom cleaner than it had ever been.

The guard came back to check on me several times. I made sure to greet him with a smile and communicate as authentically as possible how excited I was for the opportunity to clean the bathroom. Eventually he told me I had done enough, but I motioned that I would like a little more time to work on the sinks. He stared at me in disbelief.

I wish I could say my experience as a jailhouse bathroom cleaner cured my propensity for pride. It didn't. But I learned a valuable lesson, especially about how easily pride can hide from our conscious attention. If I'd been asked to rate myself on a humility scale before being approached by the guard, I would have been way too generous. Self-awareness is always difficult to cultivate—especially when it comes to pride, and perhaps especially for leaders. Pride can hide behind a leader's mask of overconfidence.

Overconfidence is rooted in pride, but it's rarely viewed as negatively by Jesus-following leaders. And overconfidence isn't just annoying to followers. It is dangerous for leaders. Malcolm Gladwell first introduced me to this idea during a lecture I attended. He said for leaders, especially in higher levels of leadership, overconfidence is a bigger problem than incompetence. There are survival-of-the-fittest forces at work in organizations that weed out chronic incompetence before it reaches high enough levels of organizational leadership to pose a big problem.

But the very same forces that weed out incompetence also feed overconfidence. Gladwell went on to say, incompetence is frustrating; overconfidence is scary.[53] It's scary because it amplifies the temptation to fall in love with our ideas and become rigid in our perspective. Overconfidence whispers into an echo chamber of subconscious thought: *You're really smart, really good at what you do, and almost always right.* The whisper is quiet at first, but even modest evidence of success amplifies the volume until we are willing to repeat this self-talk on demand.

The universal antidote for hubris is humility. And never has there been a more powerful role model of leadership humility than Jesus. As followers of Jesus, we do well to understand the subtle but dangerous ways pride hides from our consciousness and undermines our leadership.

The Leadership Conversations of Jesus

In my biblical research for this book, the biggest challenge I faced in force-ranking 1,090 leadership conversations was in how to handle the interactions of Jesus. Although often misunderstood, Jesus is the most universally respected leader of all time. No one in all of history, operating outside any organizational power structure, in such a short period of time, has had such a lasting influence. Everything Jesus said and did could rightfully be elevated to the top of any force-ranked list. I did my best to stick to the four criteria outlined in the opening chapter and landed on two leadership conversations of Jesus, which are the focus of chapters eight and nine.

The Danger of Overconfidence and Accidental Phariseeism

The leadership group most at odds with Jesus was the Pharisees. Thirty-seven of the leadership conversations of Jesus were with Pharisees or other members of the religious elite. He butted heads with them repeatedly and rebuked them powerfully, until they became obsessed with killing him. When we think of the label "Pharisee"—it always has negative connotations. But that wasn't the case during the public ministry of Jesus, as Larry Osborne writes:

> In Jesus's day, being called a Pharisee was a badge of honor. It was a compliment, not a slam.
>
> That's because first-century Pharisees excelled in everything we admire spiritually. They were zealous for God, completely committed to their faith. They were theologically astute, masters of the biblical texts. They fastidiously obeyed even the most obscure commands. They even made up extra rules just in case they were missing anything. Their embrace of spiritual disciplines was second to none.[54]

Their very piety was their problem. The Pharisees were absolutely convinced, to the point of grave overconfidence, about what they believed. And Jesus did not fit into their understanding of God's plan. The Pharisees remind us it is possible to gain the respect of followers, believe you love God and the Scriptures and try your best to live by them, and yet still be overconfidently wrong.

Only lazy, lukewarm leaders going through the motions of ministry are safe from the overconfidence of Phariseeism—as if that's any consolation. To become a modern-day Pharisee, you have to believe deeply in the kingdom work you are doing and want very much to see it grow. You have to be disciplined and prepared to sacrifice to seize opportunities before you. That's why leaders are so vulnerable. Nobody sets out to be an overconfident Pharisee. But pride is very good at hiding, often behind overconfidence. The journey to accidental Phariseeism begins with a blind spot, not a sin spot.[55]

It's true that success breeds success. But success is also a fertile breeding ground for pride, disguised as overconfidence. As a personal warning, I've kept this Dallas Willard quote in my Bible for almost a decade:

> Outward success brings a sense of accomplishment and a sense of responsibility for what has been achieved—and for further achievement.... The sense of accomplishment and responsibility reorients vision away from God to what we are doing and are to do—usually to the applause and support of sympathetic people.
>
> The ... ministry is what we spend our thoughts, feelings, and strength upon. Goals occupy the place of the vision of God in the inward life, and we find ourselves caught up in a visionless pursuit of various goals. Grinding it out. This is the point at which service to Christ replaces love for Christ.[56]

What I find especially disconcerting about the subtle drift toward the overconfidence of accidental Phariseeism is the fact it's almost never a conscious choice. Slowly, almost imperceptibly, the ministry we do for God becomes a proxy for intimacy with God. Followers can't see our hearts, only the work of our hands. When the results appear successful, the applause and support of sympathetic people may actually help us rationalize shortcuts of the heart we would never have imagined at the start. The confidence that comes with success morphs into overconfidence that serves as a mask behind which pride loves to hide.

The key question for every leader is, *How would I know if this is happening?*

I've spent a lot of time thinking about this question because I've seen this danger in my own heart. Maybe you have never struggled with this problem, and if not, pray for the rest of us. In trying to find the answer I went back to the religious leaders of Jesus' day, looking for symptoms. If they loved their positions and titles more than they loved God, even though they would never have admitted as much, what can I see in their lives as a warning sign? I found two warning signs worth mentioning: They were concerned about *survival* and *status*.

The Drive for Survival and Status

The religious leaders of Jesus's day were obsessed with survival. They wanted desperately to keep their system and power structure in place, until they were incapable of recognizing what God was doing in Jesus, right before their eyes. And that was the root of their problem. It is the same for leaders today.

The survival instinct for leaders is automatic. The more our work thrives, the more we want to protect it. That's why the first expression of groupthink in a nonprofit board is making organizational perpetuity, rather than mission effectiveness, its highest objective. These kinds of nonprofits, even faith-based ones, are like zombies. They can get scary-ugly, but they are nearly impossible to revive and hard to kill.

Don't miss the paradox: If failing to survive is not an option, then important risks will be taken off the table, which means an organization will be less likely to survive. This is the danger of marginal thinking. We see the full cost of a given risk and believe we can't afford it. But we can't calculate the true cost of *not* embracing the risk. Henry Ford said, "If you need a new machine and don't buy it, you eventually end up paying for the machine but don't have it." You're worse off than when you started.

Leaders concerned about personal survival—and none of us realize this when it's happening—attempt to prove their indispensability with lots of activity. Busyness is one of the most common ways to reinforce leadership status, so survival and status become symbiotic, to everyone's detriment. The leader thinks, *I must be important or I wouldn't be so busy.* Staying busy like the proverbial hamster racing on a wheel is somehow equated with being important.

Early in my role with The Mission Exchange (before our merger with CrossGlobal Link to form Missio Nexus), I was working more than ever and struggling to keep all the plates spinning. God led me to these words by Dallas Willard: "God never gives anyone too much to do. We do that to ourselves or we allow others to do it to us."[57]

I sensed the Holy Spirit say, "Don't blame this ridiculous pace on me."

Then, with even more conviction, "You don't trust me, and that's why you are working so hard."

When I pushed back, the Holy Spirit pressed me, "You think you can accomplish more in seven days than I can in six. That's why you don't have a Sabbath rhythm."

I experienced what it looks like to fall in love with your ministry, focus on survival, and slip into accidental Phariseeism. It rarely happens to leaders who don't care and aren't willing to work hard.

Western leaders operate in a leadership culture that worships busyness even more than results; it has become our number-one metric. Ask a successful leader how things are going, and you can expect a one-word answer: busy. Leaders who regularly take time to rest, think, and reflect are swimming against strong currents created by the culture around us.

Jesus, the Humbitious Leader

"Humbition"—a word coined by researchers at Bell Labs, is the unique blend of humility and ambition that drives most successful leaders. It serves as the antidote to the hubris that snags and then unravels far too many. Jane Harper, a longtime trainer at IBM, included the idea of humbition in a manifesto written to exhort high-potential leaders-in-training about what it takes to really succeed:

> We notice that by far the lion's share of world-changing luminaries are humble people. They focus on the work, not themselves. They seek success—they are ambitious—but they are humbled when it arrives. They know that much of that success was luck, timing, and a thousand factors out of their personal control ... Oddly, the ones operating under a delusion that they are all-powerful are the ones who have yet to reach their potential ... [So] be ambitious. Be a leader. But do not belittle others in your pursuit of your ambitions. Raise them up instead. The biggest leader is the one washing the feet of others.[58]

I love the concept of humbition. And I find it fascinating that in this manifesto of a major corporation, the metaphor of choice for humility in leadership is the example of Jesus washing the feet of his disciples.

All four Gospels reference Jesus and his disciples celebrating the Passover together. But only Luke records the conversation about leadership, triggered by the dispute among the disciples about who was the greatest. John completes the picture, giving us the demonstration of Jesus's humility as he takes up the basin and the towel.

Four Postures of Humility

Paul provides a powerful summation of the leadership style of Jesus in Philippians 2 and exhorts us to follow his example. The heading over this chapter in many Bibles says, *Imitating Christ's Humility.* Philippians 2:6–11 describes four postures of Jesus-style leadership, evidenced in his teachings and actions during the leadership conversation of the Last Supper.

No Status Belongs to Me
Paul's description of the attitude, or mindset, of Christ begins with the reminder that Jesus, "although in very nature God, did not consider equality with God something to be grasped" (Phil. 2:6). During his public ministry, Jesus—who was recognized as a religious leader—postured himself unlike other religious leaders of his day, including the Pharisees and members of the religious bureaucracy. They were obsessed with status. Jesus was not. They wanted to look important and receive recognition as such. Jesus did not.

The Gospels frequently indicated status-seeking behaviors by the Pharisees. But I'm more concerned about status-seeking signs in my life and leadership. Status has become the primary non-monetary reward for leadership.[59] Looking important is important to leaders. We have to fight this temptation every day and avoid these common status traps:

- Position: Using *where* we are on the org chart instead of *who* we are on the inside to gain influence.

- Association: Mentioning the names of other well-known leaders to boost our credibility.

- Information: Withholding what could be appropriately disclosed so that we retain power or advantage.

- Exaggeration: Overstating results to gain favor or acceptance with others, especially donors and leadership peers.

- Education: Overemphasis on what letters come after our name and which institution gave them to us.

We can be outwardly successful and zealous in defense of

orthodoxy, yet fall to the danger of accidental Phariseeism because we are totally blind to pride in our hearts. A. W. Tozer highlighted this problem with prophetic authority:

> The grosser manifestations of these sins—egotism, exhibitionism, self-promotion—are strangely tolerated in Christian leaders, even in circles of impeccable orthodoxy. They are so much in evidence as actually, for many people, to become identified with the gospel. I trust it is not a cynical observation to say that they appear these days to be a requisite for popularity in some sections of the church visible. Promoting self under the guise of promoting Christ is currently so common as to excite little notice.[60]

I confess I've struggled with all these status-seeking behaviors at one time or another. I suspect, if you are honest, you have too. Unfortunately, status-seeking behavior is easy to spot in others but difficult to see in ourselves. My observation is that everyone is against status-based leadership ... until they have status. That's what makes the example of Jesus so powerful. No leader has ever created a more status-free leadership environment than Jesus.

No Service Is Beneath Me
In Philippians 2:7, Paul continues his description of the attitude of Jesus, who "made himself nothing, taking the very nature of a servant, being made in human likeness." Jesus, in his teaching about leadership during the Last Supper, contrasted the mindset of those who lord their influence over followers with the mindset of the kingdom. He said: "But you are not to be like that. Instead, the greatest among you should be like the youngest, and the one who rules like the one who serves" (Luke 22:26).

Jesus brought this powerful, countercultural teaching to life by pouring water into a basin and washing his disciples' feet.

Symbols of status can become obstacles to service. They can get in the way of our willingness to associate with people of lower status. Elizabeth Elliot said, "The best way to find out whether you really have a servant's heart is to see what your reaction is when somebody treats you like one." That is what God was exposing in my heart when the guard asked me to clean the bathroom.

Booker T. Washington, while serving as President of the

Tuskegee Institute, was walking in town one day when he was asked by a wealthy white woman if he wanted to earn some extra money by chopping wood. Since he wasn't busy he agreed to help. One of the other servant girls working in the house recognized the man chopping wood as the president of the Tuskegee Institute. After he left, the servant girl revealed his identity to the woman.

The following day, the woman went to the Tuskegee Institute and apologized profusely for her mistake. Washington replied graciously: "It's perfectly all right, Madam. Occasionally I enjoy some manual labor. Besides, it is always a delight to do something for a friend."

That single act of humble service turned into a successful fundraiser for the Tuskegee Institute. The woman not only told her wealthy friends about Booker T. Washington's humility, but also encouraged them to join her in making generous contributions.[61]

In John's account of the Passover meal, he prefaces the description of the foot-washing by giving us a look inside the heart and mind of Jesus with these words: "Jesus knew that the Father had put all things under his power, and that he had come from God and was returning to God" (John 13:3). One of the marks of maturity is a sense of security in one's identity. Secure leaders have nothing to prove and are free to serve.

As we find our identity in Christ and join in his mission, we are recipients of his authority. When insecurity rises up within me, I try to remind myself: *The only thing I have to prove is a heart of obedience to the God who sent me.* And God always blesses obedient choices.

No Sacrifice Is Beyond Me
Paul explained that Jesus, "being found in appearance as a man, humbled himself, and became obedient to death on a cross" (Phil. 2:8)! This is the only part of the passage that includes an exclamation point. Jesus didn't die an ordinary death. He died a humiliating death on a cross.

Far too many leaders prioritize perks over sacrifice. We buy into the culture's picture of success and expect the special parking spot, the private entrance, the bigger office, and the better view. We make rules and then pretend they don't apply to us. All this has become the acceptable reward for higher levels of leadership.

As I've thought a lot about how status can impact a leader's posture toward sacrifice, I drafted a set of questions to help me evaluate the perks of leadership. Maybe you will find them helpful.

1. Do I need this—*fill in the blank*—bigger office, special parking space, or private bathroom—to do my job more effectively? Some CEOs have lots of meetings that require privacy, with individuals and with various teams. It may well be the best way to deal with this special function is to have a larger office with a meeting table. The bottom line is function. Do I need this to be more effective?

2. Is this—*fill in the blank*—a legitimate reward for my performance? Organizational cultures need not be experiments in socialism or sameness. There is nothing wrong with paying the top leader more or providing a performance-based system of motivation. Unless of course other members of the team are excluded from a properly prorated system.

3. Does this—*fill in the blank*—create distance or separation, real or perceived, between me and the people I'm leading? If your followers can't relate or connect with you, then it will be increasingly difficult to get the feedback you need. Perks reinforce the CEO bubble that hinders self-awareness. Communication channels become one-way streets, where bad news flows down, and good news flows up.

4. Does this—*fill in the blank*—increase my vulnerability to pride and egocentrism? When an organization is doing well, other people naturally want to learn why and how. This translates into visitors who even unwittingly pump the ego of a leader. Bloggers, podcasters, and publications want to tell the story. Soon there is internal pressure to make sure next year is bigger and better.

5. Would this—*fill in the blank*—make it hard for me to let go of my leadership role, even if I knew God was directing me to do so? Would I be tempted to hold on to my place of leadership in order to retain this special privilege? Few leaders readily admit how much their title and position seeps into their identity until it is time to step aside. The temptation to hold on can be stronger than you think.

It is impossible to reconcile the humble posture of Jesus with a leadership culture that craves perks and shuns sacrifice. Four words of Jesus ring in my ear when I think about all the ornaments and privileges of leadership today: *Not so with you* (Matt. 20:26). C. T. Studd, said, "If Jesus Christ be God and died for me, then no sacrifice is too great for me to make for HIM."

No Success Is Because of Me
Paul's description of the mindset of Jesus moves from humiliation to exaltation:

> Therefore God exalted him to the highest place and gave him the name that is above every name, that at the name of Jesus every knee should bow, in heaven and on earth, and every tongue confess that Jesus Christ is Lord, to the glory of God the Father (Phil. 2:10-11).

Success brings recognition. Someone has to accept the reward. The danger is believing that because you get the reward you were solely responsible for the work. Jesus shattered this mentality by saying, "I tell you the truth, the Son can do nothing by himself; he can only do what he sees the Father doing" (John 5:19). Later in the same teaching, Jesus said, "By myself I can do nothing ... for I seek not to please myself but him who sent me" (John 5:30).

There is a reward for obedience. Everything Jesus set aside when he came to earth was ultimately returned to him. And he promised that he will come for us, saying, "My reward is with me, and I will give to everyone according to what he has done" (Rev. 22:12).

I believe God rewards obedience, not results. This is not a rationalization for smallness or slothfulness in kingdom work. We should do everything we can with God's help to bear much fruit that lasts. And when we don't see the fruit we desire, we must rigorously evaluate our strategy and methods to determine if there is another approach that would yield greater fruit.

When a leader doesn't see fruit, a humble response would be to acknowledge, *It might be because of me,* and then seek every opportunity to improve. When a leader does see fruit, a humble response would be to acknowledge, *It wasn't because of me alone.* Give God glory and others praise.

Confessions and Questions to Cultivate Humble Leadership

There are a few lessons on humility we can't learn from Jesus—at least not directly. And they can be summarized in two statements, just three words each.

I was wrong.
I don't know.

Leaders who rarely say these magic words should make us nervous. The accidental Phariseeism of overconfidence won't allow a leader to accept responsibility for mistakes—full stop. Rather, there is always an explanation, a rationalization, or outright blame. It is the adult version of "the dog ate my homework," but the stakes are higher. If you have never served under or alongside a leader like this, well, as we say in the South, "God bless you." If you have served under a leader that won't say those magic words, you know how frustrating it can be.

I've discovered it is easier to admit I don't have all the answers than it is to admit some of the answers I do have are wrong. Think about that for a moment. Let it sink in. Some of my answers are wrong, I just don't know which ones. So when I discover which answers are wrong, I change them. Nobody has all the right answers. That's not as big of a problem as believing you do "have all the answers.". One of the evidences of overconfidence is an unwillingness to admit that some of our answers are wrong.

I have a special fondness for the writing of A. W. Tozer. He was a modern-day prophet who tackled hard topics head on by holding the standard of Scripture like a plumb bob, exposing warped and crooked behavior in the church. Tozer aligned himself to a high standard and called fellow leaders to do the same.

In his book, *The Pursuit of Man*, Tozer posed a series of questions that cut to the core of leadership overconfidence, which is too widely practiced and accepted in the church.

> What can we say then when Christian men vie with one another for place and position? What can we answer when we see them hungrily seeking for praise and honor? How can we excuse the passion for publicity, which is so glaringly evident among Christian leaders? What about political ambition in Church circles? What about the fevered palm that

is stretched out for more and bigger "love offerings?" What about the shameless egotism among Christians? How can we explain the gross man-worship that habitually blows up one and another popular leader to the size of colossus? What about the obsequious hand-kissing of moneyed men by those purporting to be sound preachers of the gospel?

There is only one answer to these questions, it is simply that in these manifestations we see the world and nothing but the world. No passionate profession of love for "souls" can change evil into good. These are the very sins that crucified Jesus.[62]

In this powerful and convicting statement, Tozer reminds us of the emptiness of allowing the ends to justify the means. It is tempting to believe we must be leading like Jesus—because after all, we are "growing" and our "likes" and "shares" are increasing. But Tozer reminds us that no passionate profession of a love for souls can change evil into good. Remember the lesson from chapter one: It is possible to have the power of God flowing through you without the favor of God resting on you—at least for a season.

In the opening chapter I highlighted a teaching of Jesus on leadership that is not in the Gospels. Paul quoted it to the leaders from Ephesus who attended an invitation-only meeting on the beach near Miletus: "It is more blessed to give than to receive" (Acts 20:35). Humbitious leaders want to make an impact, but not for themselves. And they never use their position of leadership for personal gain.

Humility is connected to faith and is the gateway to grace. James and John were at the center of disputes about who would have the positions of privilege beside Jesus when he came into his kingdom. But Peter may have been the disciple with the most outsized ego. He was brash, outspoken, and way overconfident.

Eventually Peter was humbled by failure and restored, which made his advice to up-and-coming leaders credible and powerful. Quoting first from Proverbs, but with the voice of personal experience, Peter said: "God opposes the proud but gives grace to the humble.' Humble yourselves, therefore, under God's mighty hand, that he may lift you up in due time" (1 Peter 5:5–6).

That's the picture of humbitious leadership, modeled by Jesus. Humility, lifted by grace, in due time.

CHAPTER 09

Mobilization

Mobilization

SPIRITUAL
LEADERSHIP ERA

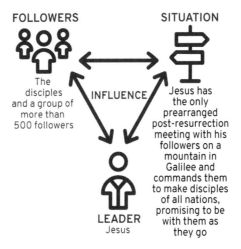

FOLLOWERS

The disciples and a group of more than 500 followers

INFLUENCE

SITUATION

Jesus has the only prearranged post-resurrection meeting with his followers on a mountain in Galilee and commands them to make disciples of all nations, promising to be with them as they go

LEADER
Jesus

"All authority in heaven and on earth has been given to me. Therefore go and make disciples of all nations, baptizing them in the name of the Father and of the Son and of the Holy Spirit, and teaching them to obey everything I have commanded you. And surely I am with you always, to the very end of the age." —Matthew 28:16–20

Executive Summary

The global body of Christ is the largest and most powerful social network in the world. One of the sparks for this movement was the leadership conversation of Jesus—known as the Great Commission. The apostles were slow to act regarding the command Jesus gave them to disciple the nations. The idea was so radical it would require a paradigm shift in their view of the Gentiles. God motivated people toward his purposes based on fear of punishment, hope of reward, and loving relationship. Understanding these motivational systems helps us mobilize followers to make disciples of all nations.

I am told I was stubborn and argumentative as a child. My response to that accusation was simple, "I am not!" My dad used to say that one day he found me a few miles from home arguing with a road sign. When he asked what I was doing I said, "This sign says it's four miles to town, and I know it's three." It never happened. But every time I'm in that area, I do take a careful look at the sign.

My own cantankerous attitude as a child—which I've long since outgrown ... wink!—has helped me reflect on the central challenge of leadership: influencing followers toward action. In chapter five I defined a leader as someone with God-given capacity and responsibility, who influences followers toward God's purpose for the group. There is a place for *thought* leadership. But the rubber meets the road when influence produces *action*.

I chose the word mobilization for this chapter because it marshals everything needed for a group to take action. Mobilization is a leadership cocktail of vision, communication, and motivation. Leaders must get followers to buy in and act out.

In the corporate world, the carrot-and-the-stick idiom often describes how leaders induce action from followers. The leader drives a cart pulled by a mule, while holding a long stick with a carrot dangling in front of the mule. Leaders constantly face choices about how best to leverage influence and incentive to keep followers moving forward, knowing that some followers will resist change because they are stubborn, opinionated, or afraid.

Jesus was the greatest leader of all time, in part because he was the greatest mobilizer of all time. Regardless of the exponential growth of technology, the global body of Christ has been and continues to be the largest and most powerful social network in the world. One of the sparks for this global movement was the leadership conversation of Jesus known as the Great Commission.

As I explained in the opening chapter of this book, the top ten leadership conversations in this book are presented in order of occurrence, not importance. If you pressed me for the most important leadership conversation out of the 1,090 identified in my research, this would be it. You might be tempted to believe my selection of the Great Commission as the number-one leadership conversation is a function of my bias for missions, based on my life experiences and career opportunities. But that's not true. All four filters in my forced ranking exercise drive this conversation to the top:

- Scope and impact
- Counterfactual questions

- Law of emphasis
- Connection to the redemption story

Careful study of the Spiritual Leadership Era reveals that the disciples were extraordinarily slow in their response to the full implication of Jesus's instructions in the Great Commission. It took almost twenty years after the ascension for the early Church to mobilize and make disciples— across significant cultural and religious boundaries. Since the first century, the body of Christ has moved back and forth on a spectrum from engagement to disengagement as it relates to our willingness to buy in and act out the instructions of Jesus to disciple the nations.

One of my favorite examples of movement toward engagement comes from the life of William Carey. In 1786, as a twenty-six-year-old pastor, William Carey attended the Ministers' Fraternal of the Northampton Association. As was the association's custom, the chairman of the meeting asked Carey to propose a question for the group to discuss. Carey had been studying the Great Commission and was confused about the way it was interpreted by leaders of his day. He asked, "whether the command given to the apostles to teach all nations was not binding on all succeeding ministers to the end of the world, seeing the accompanying promise was of equal extent."

The chairman responded, "Young man, sit down! When God pleases to converse with the heathen he'll do it without consulting you or me." William Carey sat down, but he didn't give up. Within six years he had successfully mobilized the church in England to send him as a missionary to India. He became known as the father of Protestant missions.

Advances in every endeavor require mobilization. And effective mobilization, especially in the work of the Great Commission, calls for biblical systems of motivation, which are more nuanced than the carrot-and-stick approach. By applying these systems to a contextual understanding of Jesus's leadership, we can engage more followers—and develop more leaders like William Carey—to break through barriers to the expansion of the gospel.

Putting the Great Commission in Context

The three basal elements of every leadership conversation are the leader, the followers, and the situation. Understanding the situation is critical if we are to make sense of how the leader seeks to influence followers. The Great Commission is one of a series of post-resurrection appearances of Jesus. Four contextual factors help clarify this conversation.

First, the Great Commission leadership conversation is the only such appearance that was announced in advance. Jesus wanted all of his core followers present for this important leadership conversation, unlike some of the earlier, unannounced appearances when several of the disciples were not present. For example, when Mary encountered Jesus early on the first day of the week after the crucifixion of Jesus, she wasn't expecting him and didn't recognize him, until he called her by name (John 20:10-17). The same is true for the two disciples on the road to Emmaus (Luke 24:13-32). And, more than once, Jesus suddenly appeared in a room with his disciples while they were already meeting. On one occasion, they thought he was a ghost, and he had to eat food to convince them otherwise.

In contrast to these unannounced situations, Matthew's account says, leading up to the Great Commission, "Then the eleven disciples went to Galilee, to the mountain where Jesus had told them to go" (Matt. 28:16). This was an all-hands meeting. The time and place details had been communicated in advance.

Second, the Great Commission leadership conversation is the post-resurrection appearance with the most people in attendance. Many scholars agree that Paul had this occasion in mind when stating that Jesus appeared to more than five hundred people (1 Cor. 15:6). The number is logical, given the advance announcement. The disciples were probably instructed to carefully spread the word among a larger group of followers Jesus wanted to be present.

Some evidence in Matthew's account indicates this larger group. While only eleven disciples were specifically identified, Matthew said, "When they saw him, they worshiped him, but some doubted" (Matt. 28:17). By this time the disciples had enough convincing interactions with Jesus to address their doubts. Thomas had been personally reassured, and Peter had been wonderfully restored (John 20:27, 21:15-21). It makes sense that some followers in the larger group, who were seeing Jesus for the first time after his resurrection, still had some doubts.

Third, the Great Commission is building on a previous appearance by Jesus recorded in Luke 24:36-49. Matthew does not record any significant teaching from Jesus beyond the command to make disciples of all nations. Jesus had already given his disciples the backstory.

Luke records that Jesus explained, "Everything must be fulfilled that is written about me in the Law of Moses, the Prophets, and the Psalms" (Luke 24:44). Jesus went on to open the minds of the disciples so they could understand the Scriptures, including this Old Testament prophecy:

> The Christ will suffer and rise from the dead on
> the third day, and repentance and forgiveness of
> sins will be preached in his name to all nations,
> beginning in Jerusalem (Luke 24:46–47).

It is beyond the scope of this book, but I would love to take you back into the Old Testament stories of the Patriarchal Leadership Era to demonstrate how the mobilization focus of Jesus in the Great Commission was not a new idea at all. Rather, it was the fulfillment of God's promise that through Abraham he would bless all the peoples of the earth.

Missiologists point out that when Jesus said to make disciples of all "nations," he wasn't referring to geopolitical units on a map. He was referring to ethnolinguistic people groups, as referenced in Revelation when representatives "from every tribe and language and people and nation" will sing a new song of worship to the Lamb who sits on the throne (Rev. 4:9).

Finally, the fourth contextual factor in the Great Commission leadership conversation is its distinct separateness from the ascension. The Great Commission happened on a mountain in Galilee where Jesus had instructed his followers to go. The ascension happened on the Mount of Olives, which is not in Galilee. My reason for pointing this out is to reinforce the fact that the Great Commission was not a spiritual postscript on the interaction of Jesus with his followers. He didn't give the charge to disciple the nations and then slip off into the clouds. His final command wasn't to go, but rather to wait in Jerusalem for the promised gift of the Holy Spirit, who would give them the power to be his witnesses all the way to the ends of the earth.

Putting the Great Commission into Action

The apostles, who first followed Jesus as a Jewish rabbi, were slow to act regarding his command to disciple the nations, even after the birth of the Church through the outpouring of the Holy Spirit. The idea required a radical shift in their view of the Gentiles.

But the gospel gained momentum during the first century like an epic symphony or movie soundtrack, with five movements building in succession.

Jews and Proselytes to Judaism (Acts 2)

Peter emerged as the mouthpiece for the gospel on the day of Pentecost to the Jews gathered in Jerusalem "from every nation under heaven." Gentiles joined the gathering too, drawn by the highly ethical and monotheistic faith of Judaism, which they had discovered in synagogues, formed among the Jewish diaspora. Some of these Gentile proselytes were willing to be circumcised and baptized, and to live according to the Mosaic Law. Luke records that about three thousand people accepted Peter's message and were baptized that day (Acts 2:11,41).

Samaritans (Acts 8)

Some scholars have traced the bad blood between Jews and Samaritans to more than one thousand years before Jesus. The disciples were not immune to Jewish prejudice and hatred toward Samaritans as half-breed Jews with a distorted understanding of how to worship God. Samaritans were the social equals of stray dogs. Jews went out of their way to avoid contact with them whenever possible. That's why it was so startling for the disciples when Jesus "had to go through Samaria," which led to his encounter with the woman at the well (John 4:4). When the people in a Samaritan village were slow to welcome Jesus, both James and John wanted to call down fire from heaven to destroy them.

This context helps us understand why it was a significant first step in responding to the Great Commission when Philip "went down to a city in Samaria and proclaimed the Christ there" (Acts 8:5). Philip's ministry was miraculous and fruitful, bringing "great joy in that city" (Acts 8:8). When word of Philip's ministry reached Jerusalem, Peter and John were sent to see for themselves, then joined the ministry by "preaching the gospel in many Samaritan villages" (Acts 8:25).

God-Fearing Gentiles (Acts 10)

Some of the Gentiles drawn to Judaism were unwilling to be circumcised and baptized, or to live under the Mosaic Law. They participated on the margins of synagogue life and did their best to follow the ways of God. The Hebrew Scriptures had been translated into Greek, giving non-Jews access to the stories and ways of God.

One of these God-fearers, Cornelius, served as a centurion in the Italian Regiment, based in Caesarea. "He and all his family were devout and God-fearing; he gave generously to those in need and prayed to God regularly" (Acts 10:2). The amazing story of how God brought Peter to Cornelius's house is worth more time than can be devoted here. At its heart, this passage reveals God's exposure of Peter's unbiblical perspective on the Gentiles. Peter ultimately confessed to Cornelius and his extended family and friends, "I now realize how true it is that God does not show favoritism but accepts men from every nation who fear him and do what is right" (Acts 10:34).

Peter, one of the inner-circle disciples, had to go on a short-term mission trip to Joppa and look Gentiles in the eye to understand what Jesus had been saying all along. Peter's subsequent decision to baptize Cornelius and his household stirred the controversy and opposition when Peter returned to Jerusalem. The circumcised believers "criticized him and said, 'You went into the house of uncircumcised men and ate with them" (Acts 11:3). Peter defended his actions by explaining the supernatural ways God had directed him. He said, "Who was I to think I could oppose God" (Acts 11:17)?

Pagan Gentiles (Acts 11)

A persecution broke out in Jerusalem against the followers of Jesus, which scattered them throughout Judea and Samaria (Acts 8:1). This turn of events provided part of the impetus that brought Philip to the Samaritans. Among the believers who had scattered were men from Cyprus and Cyrene. They went to Antioch and began to speak to pagan Gentiles, " ... telling them the good news about the Lord Jesus. The Lord's hand was with them, and a great number of people believed and turned to the Lord" (Acts 11:20-21).

This movement of God in Antioch is the first intentional cross-cultural disciple-making activity in the book of Acts. When word of it reached Jerusalem, some followers of Jesus must have expressed suspicion about the legitimacy of the ministry. Barnabas was sent to Antioch to inspect the fruit. "When he arrived he saw the evidence of the grace of God, he was glad and encouraged them all to remain true to the Lord with all their hearts" (Acts 11:23). I don't want to read into the text, but it appears Barnabas had advised the Antioch believers of the suspicion in Jerusalem regarding the legitimacy of their faith. Perhaps he didn't want the Gentile believers to give the Jewish believers any reason to doubt.

Barnabas was giving leadership to an exploding movement of disciples in Antioch. He needed help. But there wasn't a long line of Jewish leaders looking for assignments among Gentiles. Barnabas went looking for the one person he knew had been called for this kind of cross-cultural ministry: Saul, who would later be called Paul.

After Saul's conversion on the road to Damascus, he visited Jerusalem. But believers there shunned him because of his history as a religious terrorist, bent on killing followers of Jesus. Only Barnabas, who had direct access to the apostles, was willing to take a chance on Saul. No doubt when Saul told Barnabas about his time in Damascus, he explained that Ananias said he would be God's "chosen instrument to carry my name before the Gentiles and their kings and before the people of Israel" (Acts 9:15). Yet some Jews in Jerusalem reacted violently to Saul's teaching about Jesus, so believers sent him home to Tarsus.

Saul had been out of the mix for about ten years when Barnabas came knocking on his door with an invitation to serve among Gentiles in Antioch. This would prove to be the ideal place for Paul to learn under Barnabas for a year, meeting with the church and teaching great numbers of people (Acts 11:26).

Cyprus and Beyond (Acts 13)

The disciple-making movement in Antioch, the first among pagan Gentiles, became the ideal launching pad for the broader mission activity of the early Church. Their commitment to send and support the mission of Paul brought to life a fully orbed obedience to the Great Commission leadership conversation of Jesus.

It began in a meeting with a culturally diverse group of spiritual leaders:

> While they were worshiping the Lord and fasting, the Holy Spirit said, "Set apart for me Barnabas and Saul for the work to which I have called them." (Acts 13:2)

The spiritual center of gravity in the early Church began to shift from Jerusalem to Antioch, and the Scriptures began to speak of Paul, rather than Saul. Jerusalem remained the administrative hub, but Antioch became the missional hub, from which Paul would embark on his missionary journeys.

Within four years, "all the Jews and Greeks who lived in the province of Asia heard the word of the Lord" (Acts 19:10).

Through the Great Commission, Jesus became the greatest mobilizer of all time. The movement he began, though small at the start, continues to swell in ever-increasing movements of the gospel that reach tens of thousands every day. But there is no denying it took nearly twenty years, after three years of intensive training, for his followers to fully embrace the vision he put before them. And in the earliest stages of living this vision from the sending base in Antioch, heated controversy required a major leadership meeting in Jerusalem (Acts 15). But that's the subject of the next chapter.

Three Biblical Systems of Motivation

Influence that leads to action is at the heart of leadership. I'm using mobilization as the umbrella label because it incorporates the leadership functions that produce action. Let's take a closer look at the three motivational systems used in the Bible by God to mobilize people toward his purposes.

Throughout the Bible we see evidence of God motivating people toward his purposes based on (1) fear of punishment, (2) hope of reward, and (3) loving relationship.[63] Understanding these motivational systems helps us make wise decisions about how to mobilize followers—as we run our part of the spiritual relay race through history to make disciples of all nations.

Fear of Punishment

Moses introduced the plagues God brought upon Egypt by saying: "Let my people go, so that they may worship me. If you refuse to let them go, I will ..." (Ex. 8:1–2, 9:1–2, 13–14, 10:3–4). Moses then described each plague intended to punish Pharaoh for his hardness of heart.

Even the social laws governing Israel included motivation based on the fear of punishment. "Anyone who strikes a man and kills him shall surely be put to death" (Ex. 21:12). "A thief must certainly make restitution.... If the stolen animal is found alive in his possession ... he must pay back double" (Ex. 22:3–4).

Moses also warned the Israelites:

> If you ever forget the Lord your God and follow other gods and worship and bow down to them, I testify against you today that you will surely be destroyed (Deut. 8:19).

Scripture includes many other warnings by the prophets, who spoke as representatives of God, seeking to motivate the people toward God's purposes for the group.

John the Baptist prepared the way for Jesus by preaching a message of repentance that included a fear of punishment motivation. Speaking of Jesus, John said:

> But after me will come one who is more powerful than I, whose sandals I am not fit to carry. He will baptize you with the Holy Spirit and with fire. His winnowing fork is in his hand, and he will clear his

threshing floor, gathering his wheat into the barn
and burning up the chaff with unquenchable fire
(Matt. 3:11–12).

Jesus told his disciples:

Things that cause people to sin are bound to come,
but woe to that person through whom they come.
It would be better for him to be thrown into the
sea with a millstone tied around his neck than for
him to cause one of these little ones to sin. So watch
yourselves (Luke 17:1–3).

Hope of Reward

Moses received a message from God on Mount Sinai even before he
was given the Ten Commandments. God told him to tell the people,
"If you obey me fully and keep my covenant, then out of all nations
you will be my treasured possession" (Ex. 19:5).

In some cases, the hope of reward was used alongside fear
of punishment as a basis for motivation. Most notably, these two
systems were combined in Moses's farewell message to Israel, as
blessings for obedience and curses for disobedience (Deut. 28).
Moses began, "If you fully obey the LORD your God and carefully
follow all his commands I give you today..." Then he continued with
a description of the fruits of obedience that come with God's lavish
blessing. Next came the warning about disobedience—"However, if
you do not fully obey the LORD your God and do not carefully follow
all his commands ..."—which was followed by a detailed explanation
of the folly of life outside God's blessing.

Jesus didn't shy away from using the hope of reward as a
motivational system. He told his disciples that "anyone who
receives a prophet because he is a prophet will receive a prophet's
reward." He went on to say that "even a cup of cold water" given
to his disciples would be rewarded (Matt. 10:41–42). Some of the
final words of Jesus, recorded by John in Revelation, say, "Behold I
am coming soon! My reward is with me, and I will give to everyone
according to what he has done" (Rev. 22:12).

Loving Relationship

Jesus elevated the words of Moses by identifying the greatest
commandment in the Law: "Love the Lord your God with all your
heart and with all your soul and with all your mind." This love for

God would fuel the second greatest commandment to "Love your neighbor as yourself" (Matt. 22:37–39). Jesus gave direct and explicit instructions to his disciples, saying, "If you love me, you will obey what I command" (John 14:15).

Applying the Best System of Motivation

Since all three of these motivational systems are used in the Bible, a leadership and mobilization question worth asking is: Which system is the best? The intuitive response would favor loving relationship. But the best approach is more nuanced, depending on the maturity of the person you are trying to motivate and the nature of the task you want them to accomplish.

Imagine a conversation with your five-year-old child about riding her bike. If you want to motivate your daughter to stay away from the danger of riding in the street, you aren't going to say, *If you love Mommy and Daddy, you won't ride your bike in the street.* The conversation will be more like: *Mommy and Daddy love you very much. We don't want you to get hurt, and riding your bike in the street isn't safe. You can ride freely in the driveway, but if you go in the street I'll put your bike away until tomorrow.*

Now fast forward to the day she goes off to college. You will have another conversation about what you expect, but it will bend toward loving relationship because of the developing maturity of a young adult.

Jesus did not use the loving relationship motivational approach indiscriminately with the masses. It was to his disciples, in the final stages of his ministry, that he said, "If you love me, you will obey what I command" (John 14:15).

How Motivation Can Make or Break Mobilization

What does all this have to do with the leadership conversation of the Great Commission, and how does it apply to leaders today? Let me try to connect the dots.

You can't mobilize people effectively to make disciples of all nations using only fear of punishment or hope of reward. The nature of the task calls for maturing disciples, based on a loving relationship. But immature followers will not respond consistently to the motivation of a loving relationship. This is a proverbial catch-22 for spiritual leaders seeking to mobilize followers to fulfill the Great Commission.

For those who are early in their journey of following Jesus, the best system of motivation combines fear of punishment with hope of reward. The writer of Hebrews expressed frustration and disappointment regarding those who "need milk" like an infant instead of "solid food" that nourishes those who are more mature (Heb. 5:13–14). Similarly, this exhortation continues with a farming metaphor that contrasts the opportunity for blessing and the danger of being cursed:

> Land that drinks in the rain often falling on it and that produces a crop useful to those for whom it is farmed receives the blessing of God. But land that produces thorns and thistles is worthless and is in danger of being cursed. In the end it will be burned (Heb. 6:7–9).

Leaders face a problem when mobilizing followers to buy in and act out the Great Commission: Hidden biases keep people from engaging those who are not like them. Success demands overcoming this problem and breaking down prejudice through a maturing love relationship with God. The problem and the solution are not new. Hidden biases of early Church leaders slowed the initial spread of the gospel. Peter admitted in his meeting with Cornelius's household that only in that moment did he realize "God did not show favoritism," but accepted people from every nation (Acts 10:34).

It would be naïve for us to believe that leaders and followers today are exempt from these sinful attitudes or that prejudice doesn't play a role in holding back the wave of workers needed to run our leg of the race, circling the globe with the gospel message. The call to leave what is familiar and risk rejection or persecution is fueled by the love of Christ that compels us into service (2 Cor. 5:14). This is not the behavior of infants coddled on milk.

As it relates to the Great Commission, far too many followers are not mature enough to be motivated by a love relationship, which is the only effective fuel for taking up this challenge. Therein lies our mobilization challenge as leaders. And add to it another layer of complexity that relates to our misunderstanding of spiritual maturity. We can't develop what we haven't properly defined.

Redefining Spiritual Maturity

Modern-day Christianity, especially in the Western Church, has embraced a knowledge-based definition of spiritual maturity. We look to those who know a lot about the Bible or have a lot experience with the institution of the local church and assume they are spiritually mature, without any serious consideration of how readily they act on what they know.

We have venerated knowledge to the point where the only action required is to show up at the next training seminar. Notebooks from the seminar find their place on our shelf like a spiritual merit badge. Unfortunately, the knowledge is also put on the shelf.

But Jesus measured maturity by a person's obedience, not knowledge. This is the entire point of the story he told in Luke 6:46–49, about the wise and foolish builders. Both builders heard Jesus's words. The wise one put them into practice, while the foolish one did not. The fates of their respective houses serve to illustrate the presence of maturity and the lack of maturity. The houses looked the same on the outside. But one stood while the other fell when the storms of life swept over them.

A biblical understanding of spiritual maturity is not based on knowledge but on the size of the gap between knowledge and obedience. A Jesus-follower with limited knowledge that is matched by obedience is more mature than a person with lots of knowledge but little obedience.

The Western Church often marvels at stories of newfound faith in other parts of the world that include powerful witness or miraculous signs and wonders. How can people with so little training or knowledge be so powerfully used by God? Some rationalize the answer by explaining their worldview is more open to the spirit world. Others reference their lack of modern medical facilities.

But there is another, more compelling explanation. When the gap between knowledge and obedience is small, faith and spiritual power become great. And when the gap between knowledge and obedience is large, faith and spiritual power remain small. Sadly, it is possible to have a form of godliness with no power (2 Tim. 3:5).

A. W. Tozer pushed back against this hypocrisy, saying, "Salvation apart from obedience is unknown in the sacred scriptures." Dallas Willard went even farther, calling it heresy:

> This 'heresy' has created the impression that it is quite reasonable to be a 'vampire Christian.' One in effect says to Jesus, 'I'd like a little of your blood please. But I don't care to be your student or have your character. In fact, won't you just excuse me while I get on with my life, and I'll see you in heaven.' But can we really imagine that this is an approach that Jesus finds acceptable?[64]

Research about the Church in North America reveals how little those who claim to follow Jesus know about the Bible. It is disconcerting. But it is less problematic than the lack of obedience to what we do know. There is a ceiling on spiritual formation that knowledge cannot break through. In fact, without obedience, more knowledge only compounds the hypocrisy.

The fastest growing discipleship movements today are spreading because ordinary people are encountering Jesus and, from the beginning of their faith walk, they are expected to *do* what they *know*. Discovery Bible study groups often support their growth by focusing on very simple questions: What is God saying to you? What are you going to do about it? Everyone in the group is expected to support knowledge with action. And because the gap between knowledge and obedience is small, spiritual power is great, and miracles are common.

Integrating Discipleship and Missions

The mobilization challenge, especially as it relates to the Great Commission, requires a love-relationship motivation that reinforces the teachings of Jesus, who said: "If you love me, you will obey what I command." Jesus-followers who are still feeding on milk—or in the words of Dallas Willard, who embrace vampire Christianity—cannot be motivated effectively by a love relationship.

So now what?

The spiritual formation department of the local church needs the ministry formation department and vice versa—just like the right hand needs the left. Spiritual practices that cultivate intimacy and godly character must integrate with acts of service that put giftedness to good work. It's not a matter of one first, then the other. The two work in tandem. It is wise to withhold leadership from new Jesus-followers. It is not wise to withhold service from anyone. Spiritual formation and ministry formation are organically connected. Embedded in the Great Commission is the command to "teach them to obey everything I have commanded you." Mobilizing Jesus-followers to get on mission is part of what is required to help them grow.

Avoiding Spiritual #FOMO

In my mobilization efforts, I've looked for creative ways to combine all three systems of biblical motivation. One of the passages that prompted my integrated approach is Matthew 24:12–14. Inserted into his teaching on the end of the age, Jesus said:

Because of the increase of wickedness, the love of most will grow cold, but he who stands firm to the end will be saved. And this gospel of the kingdom will be preached as a testimony to all nations, and then the end will come.

There is disagreement among mission leaders regarding the interpretation of this passage. We can say with confidence that at some point, the end will come. And before that time, the gospel will be preached to all nations. Some generation of Jesus-followers will run the anchor leg in the Great Commission relay race of history. But every generation should live as if the baton of responsibility for world evangelization has been passed to them for the final lap.

How sad would it be to get to heaven and discover God had chosen your generation to run the anchor leg and bring the gospel to the nations before the end would come, only to realize you missed out on the excitement? We are used to seeing #FOMO—fear of missing out—as a hashtag on far more trivial matters. But this fear goes farther than trendy shorthand. As we mobilize to fulfill the Great Commission, leaders and followers can find motivation based on the fear of missing out on a blessing of an eternal reward.

And how would people be in danger of missing out? By allowing their love relationship with God to grow cold.

CHAPTER 10

Judgment

Judgment

SPIRITUAL
LEADERSHIP ERA

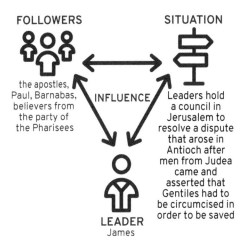

FOLLOWERS

the apostles,
Paul, Barnabas,
believers from
the party of
the Pharisees

INFLUENCE

SITUATION

Leaders hold
a council in
Jerusalem to
resolve a dispute
that arose in
Antioch after
men from Judea
came and
asserted that
Gentiles had to
be circumcised in
order to be saved

LEADER
James

"It is my judgment, therefore, that we should not make it difficult
for the Gentiles who are turning to God." —Acts 15:19

Executive Summary

One of the distinctives of leadership is the number of high-level
decisions that come with the territory. Judgment and influence are
directly related. The more influence you have, the more important
your judgment because the outcome affects more people. Judgments
about people, strategy, and crisis have the greatest impact on the
survival and vitality of any organization. The Jerusalem Council is
one of the highest stakes meetings in the New Testament because it
includes all three. When making judgments, wise leaders prioritize
discerning the voice of God in the Word, the heart, the church, and
in the circumstances.

What is the most important decision you've ever made? How about the top five? How did they turn out? If you interview leaders in the final stages of life, the answers to these three questions will tell you a lot about their legacy. That's because the legacy of leaders, and the success of the organizations they lead, will be determined by the cumulative outcome of their most important judgment calls. The chapters in our leadership biography will be organized around the key judgments we make.

At any stage of life, if you reflect on the most important decisions you've made so far, you will likely find several that disproportionately affect the quality and trajectory of your journey. For me, one of those pivot-point decisions was about which Bible college to attend. I had made my decision, applied and been accepted, sorted out my financial aid, registered for classes, secured housing, and literally packed my car. I was planning to leave the following morning. But something just didn't feel right.

I called my pastor and asked if I could come see him. We spent about an hour processing the factors affecting my decision. By the time we closed our meeting with prayer, I knew I would be exploring another option. Within a week I was headed to a university in Canada, instead of the one I had been expecting to attend in a suburb of Philadelphia. There was nothing wrong with the college I decided not to attend. But the judgment call to take a different path ultimately connected me with the mission trip I've written about in previous chapters and with the woman I would marry. It changed the trajectory of my life in ways I could never have understood at the time.

If you google how many choices are made in a day, the most likely answer is 35,000. But this question is impossible to answer. One of the scientific studies on this topic comes from Cornell University where researchers determined we make an average of 226.7 decisions per day about food alone.[65] Is that number precise enough for you? Maybe life really is like a box of chocolates.

Most of the decisions we make are trivial. People who consistently get ordinary decisions wrong are said to be lacking in common sense. My grandfather's favorite idiom for this kind of person was, "He doesn't even know enough to get out of the rain." Maybe you've met some people like that. I confess I heard my grandfather use this idiom about me more than once. But there is another level of decision-making associated with a more important category of choices. People who consistently get these higher-level decisions wrong are said to have bad judgment.

How Decisions Define a Leadership Legacy

One of the distinctives of leadership is the number of high-level decisions that come with the territory. In the book *Judgment* by Noel Tichy and Warren Bennis, the authors assert: "The single most important thing leaders do is make good judgment calls." They go on to say, "With good judgment, little else matters. Without it, *nothing* else matters."[66] Judgment and influence are directly related. The more influence you have, the more important your judgment because the outcome of your decision-making affects a larger number of people.

Acts 15 records one of the highest stakes meetings in the Church sub-phase of the Spiritual Leadership Era. Because of its significance, it became known as the Jerusalem Council. The apostles—along with Paul, Barnabas, and a delegation of leaders from the church at Antioch— attended this important meeting. They convened in response to a group of leaders from Judea who had come to Antioch and begun teaching the Gentile converts: "Unless you are circumcised, according to the custom taught by Moses, you cannot be saved" (Acts 15:1).

Paul and Barnabas had been helping lead the church at Antioch and strongly disagreed with this message. Apparently, the Judean leaders claimed they had the backing from the Church leaders in Jerusalem, so Paul, Barnabas, and the Antioch delegation traveled to Jerusalem to settle the matter. The future of Christianity would hinge on the judgment call coming out of their meeting. A mere twenty-five years after the resurrection of Christ, the stakes could not be higher for the young movement he had commissioned to the ends of the earth.

We can learn much from how the early Church leaders handled this important conversation. We'll get the benefit of hindsight from the foresight they demonstrated at the Jerusalem Council, especially as we understand three categories of judgment calls we must make well if we are to be effective leaders.

Three Domains of Leadership Judgment

Noel Tichy and Warren Bennis advocate that leaders must exercise good judgment about *people, strategy,* and *crisis.*[67] Of the thousands of decisions leaders make every day, judgments in these three domains will have the greatest impact on the survival and vitality of any organization.

People judgments are the most common, important, and complex of the three domains. Leaders make critical decisions about whom they will hire, what role each person will fill, and how to help a group become a high-functioning team. People judgments can be affected by emotional attachments among team members and in their individual relationships with the leader. When leaders don't get people judgments right, they will find it difficult to pursue a wise strategy and will eventually create a crisis.

Strategy ultimately boils down to the choices leaders make that give direction to their team about the best way to pursue the vision and mission God has entrusted to them. Some ministry leaders have been inclined to relegate strategy to the world of business. That in itself is a judgment. Choosing not to actively develop a strategy is, in my judgment, a bad strategy.

Jesus made strategy judgments based on his mission all the time. On one occasion, the people of Capernaum went looking for Jesus, who had gone to a solitary place in the morning to pray. He had been healing people and casting out demons, which drew even larger crowds who wanted help. When they found Jesus, they tried to keep him from leaving them, but he responded with a strategic ministry priority: "I must preach the good news of the kingdom of God to the other towns also, because that is why I was sent" (Luke 4:42–43). It would be easy to understand the judgment call Jesus made to leave Capernaum if the people were unresponsive. But he said no to their request, based on his mission.

Crisis judgments and their results are often amplified by the time-sensitivity associated with the decision-making cycle. Crisis reveals the strength or weakness of systems for gathering input, communicating with stakeholders, and executing with precision. Under duress, any unsteadiness in the leader as it relates to values can cloud judgment and inflate the importance of short-term results. But a wise leader leans into values and handles crisis decisions with a long-term view.

The Jerusalem Council in Acts 15 included all three domains of leadership judgment. It involved people—non-Jewish followers of Jesus, and what would be required of them to gain acceptance in the early Church. It involved strategy, especially for Paul and Barnabas, who had already completed their first missionary journey with an increasing focus on Gentiles. And it involved a pending crisis for Gentile followers of Jesus in Antioch, whom Barnabas had affirmed more than two years earlier when he visited them. Barnabas had been sent by the Jerusalem church to inspect the spiritual fruit of ministry in Antioch and had reported upon arriving that he "saw evidence of the grace of God" (Acts 11:23).

The Judgment Call at the Jerusalem Council

Sometimes the stakes surrounding a leadership judgment are so high and the issues so complex, that the only way to resolve the problem is to get everyone in the same room. That was the case with the Jerusalem Council.

James, the brother of Jesus, chaired the meeting and carried the weight of the judgment. The apostles attended—minus James, the brother of John, who had been beheaded by King Herod. Paul, Barnabas, and a delegation of leaders from Antioch were also present, along with believers who belonged to the party of the Pharisees—the same group whose teaching in Antioch brought the crisis to the surface. Luke refers to the entire group as an assembly, so it is possible there were others from Jerusalem attending who are not specifically identified.

This assembly of leaders focused on a central question: Do Gentile believers have to be circumcised and live culturally as Jews under the Law of Moses to be saved? After much discussion about the question, Peter stepped forward to address the group. He reminded them of his God-prompted visit to the house of Cornelius, the God-fearing Gentile in Caesarea. God demonstrated his acceptance of Gentiles by "giving the Holy Spirit to them, just as he did to us," Peter said (Acts 15:8). He asserted that the yoke of the law was too heavy for anyone to bear, and it was "through the grace of our Lord Jesus that we are saved, just as they are" (Acts 15:11).

Next, Barnabas and Paul recounted "the miraculous signs and wonders God had done among the Gentiles through them" (Acts 15:12). After they finished, James referenced the words of the prophet Amos, who spoke about the rebuilding of David's tent:

> Its ruins I will rebuild, and I will restore it, that
> the remnant of men may seek the Lord, and all the
> Gentiles who bear my name, says the Lord.... (Acts
> 15:16–17, Amos 9:11–12)

Then James made the hard call: "It is my judgment, therefore, that we should not make it difficult for the Gentiles who are turning to God" (Acts 15:19). It would be hard to overstate the significance of this leadership judgment in resolving a crisis and continuing to engage people and implement strategy in the spread of the gospel.

A Framework for Good Judgment

For Jesus-following leaders there is no substitute for the voice of

God in making judgment calls. No data point is more critical for any decision, whether about people, strategy, or crisis, than the wisdom of God. The question is, "How can I reliably hear the voice of God in decision-making?" There is no magic formula, but I've found a helpful framework evidenced in the Acts 15 account of the Jerusalem Council. My leadership mentor, Bobby Clinton—who credits his professor at Columbia International University, "Buck" Hatch—first introduced me to this framework.[68]

Judgment Framework

Hearing the Voice of God in the Heart	Hearing the Voice of God in the Church / Community	Hearing the Voice of God in the Circumstances
[Inner Peace]	[Godly Counsel]	[Open & Closed Doors]

Hearing the Voice of God in the Word

The foundation of the framework is hearing the voice of God in the Word. God will never direct us toward action that is inconsistent with what he has already revealed in the Bible. The more we engage the Bible, the more familiar we become with God's values and his voice. If you want to grow in your ability to recognize the voice of God in the prompts of daily life, spend more time engaging his Word.

Resting on this foundational element we can hear God's voice in three equally valid sources: the heart, the church, and the circumstances. The voice of God in the heart is often called *inner peace*. This can be hard to describe, but you have probably heard people say, *I just don't have peace about it.* Early on in my own journey, it seemed easier for me to recognize the lack of peace about a judgment than the presence of peace. Over time, I'm settled in my ability to recognize both.

The voice of God in the church represents the input of godly counsel from trusted and wise people. Every Jesus-following leader needs a core advisory group of like-minded people of faith. And leaders will often find it helpful, even necessary, to seek input from subject-matter experts outside the community of faith.

The voice of God in circumstances represents the way God opens and closes doors to help give us guidance. This aspect of the framework requires discernment. Are closed doors due to the Enemy blocking our way? Or is God redirecting our path? As we consider these questions, we must rely on all four aspects of the judgment framework, working together to help us make a high-stakes decision.

At the Jerusalem Council, James laid a foundation for his judgment by asserting, "The words of the prophets are in agreement with this," before quoting Amos specifically. This is the voice of God in the Word. The entire assembly of leaders represented a diversity of voices capable of providing wise counsel. And the specific testimonies of Peter, Barnabas, and Paul provided evidence from circumstances that God was not only opening the door to the Gentiles but blessing the ministry among them without preconditions.

After James made the judgment call, "the apostles and elders, with the whole church, decided to choose some of their own men and send them to Antioch with Paul and Barnabas" (Acts 15:22). The council leaders endorsed the delegation with a letter from the leaders that would provide final clarity about the judgment call they had made. In the letter, an interesting phrase beautifully reflects the inner peace aspect of the framework for good judgment: "It seemed good to the Holy Spirit and to us ..." (Acts 15:28). When our hearts and minds are in sync with the Holy Spirit, it seems good, and provides a sense of inner peace.

Three Steps Forward, Two Steps Back

Paul, Barnabas, and the Antioch delegation left Jerusalem with both a letter and witnesses that affirmed the decision to not make it difficult for Gentiles who were turning to God. This resolved the issue once and for all. Until it didn't. A hiccup occurred sooner than anyone expected and from a most unlikely source.

Peter followed Paul and Barnabas to Antioch sometime after the Jerusalem Council.[69] Paul referenced this visit in his letter to the church at Galatia, explaining that before certain men came from Jerusalem to Antioch:

> [Peter] used to eat with the Gentiles. But when the group from Jerusalem arrived, Peter drew back and separated himself from the Gentiles. He was afraid of those who belonged to the circumcision group. The other Jews joined him in his hypocrisy, so that by their hypocrisy even Barnabas was led astray (Gal. 2:11–13).

The Jerusalem Council had squarely addressed the issue of what should not be expected of non-Jews. However, what it did not clarify directly was how much freedom Jews should have with regard to the dietary regulations in the Mosaic law. Jews had for centuries separated themselves from Gentiles for meals. This is why Peter's actions in Acts 10 were so controversial: "You went into the house of uncircumcised men and ate with them" (Acts 11:3). Peter appears to have vacillated by eating with Gentiles in Antioch when none of the strict Jews from Jerusalem were present and by refraining when the Jews arrived.

Paul saw Peter's actions as violating the truth of the gospel and confronted him publicly. Paul's concern was not primarily about Peter's eating habits but rather about the message he was sending to the Gentile believers. Paul spoke to him in front of everyone: "You are a Jew, yet you live like a Gentile and not like a Jew. How is it, then, that you force Gentiles to follow Jewish customs" (Gal. 2:14)?

The twist in the story is important because it shows us that even the best leaders are capable of bad judgment right on the heels of good judgment—even about the same issue. Strong-willed and self-assured leaders like Peter can still bend to the poor judgment of people around them. Other factors such as our values and worldview also affect our judgment. That's where the narrative about judgment in Acts 15 gets even more interesting.

Paul, Barnabas, and Their Differing Judgments about John Mark

Enter John Mark—his Hebrew name was John and his Roman name was Mark. His presence is a possible clue that Peter visited Antioch soon after the Jerusalem Council. John Mark surfaced again in Antioch and was closely influenced by Peter. It is widely held that the Gospel according to Mark was based largely on information from Peter. It is likely that Peter brought John Mark with him when he made his visit to Antioch.

When Paul sensed it was time to launch a second missionary journey, Barnabas wanted to take John Mark along. Paul didn't. He had a sharp disagreement with Barnabas about a people judgment. Paul felt it was unwise because John Mark had deserted them on the first journey. Barnabas wouldn't back down, so Paul and Barnabas parted company—in sharp disagreement.

Judgments of every kind—people, strategy, and crisis—are affected in ways we might not expect. The information we gather about any judgment is always interpreted through hidden filters, such as our values and worldview. Such was the case with John Mark.

The Backstory on John Mark's Failed Internship

We could describe John Mark's experience as a failed internship. And while it may seem like a detour, an exploration of the backstory with Paul and Barnabas helps explain how these two leaders, with such a rich history, could disagree so sharply about John Mark.

The opportunity for John Mark to intern with Barnabas and Saul, as he was still known at the time, began when Peter was put in prison. The church had gathered at the house of John Mark's mother, Mary, to pray for Peter (Acts 12:12). Barnabas and Saul had come to Jerusalem around the same time, to deliver a gift to the elders, in response to the prophecy given by Agabus about the famine that would affect the entire Roman world (Acts 11:27–30). Barnabas was Mary's brother[70] and thereby John Mark's uncle, so if Barnabas was in town during the time of the prayer meeting, you can presume he and Saul would have been at her house too.

It is possible that Saul met John Mark for the first time during this visit, perhaps at the prayer meeting itself. How ever their paths crossed, "when Barnabas and Saul had finished their mission, they returned from Jerusalem, taking with them John, also called Mark" (Acts 12:25). So John Mark traveled with his uncle Barnabas, as well as Barnabas's ministry assistant, Saul, to the city of Antioch. When John Mark signed on to travel with them to Antioch, he had no way of knowing that the Holy Spirit was about to interrupt a leadership team meeting saying, "Set apart Barnabas and Saul for the work to which I have called them" (Acts 13:2).

Questions have been raised as to how specifically the itinerary of this missionary journey was planned beyond the initial stop on the island of Cyprus. Some have suggested that the phrase, "the work they had now completed," in Acts 14:26, demonstrates a well-defined plan. But in Paul's first epistle—written to churches started during this journey—he seems to indicate otherwise. It states that he visited the region of Galatia due to an illness and not a predetermined plan (Gal. 4:13).

The point is that John Mark probably accepted the opportunity to travel with Barnabas and Saul to Cyprus, which was Barnabas's home, without fully understanding where they would go next. And it is also understandable why he would not want to remain in Antioch without the people who brought him from Jerusalem.

After arriving in Cyprus, " ... they traveled through the whole island until they came to Paphos" (Acts 13:6). That's when things began to change. Barnabas had been the distinct leader of the group in Jerusalem, where he had all the connections and positive history with the apostles. Remember, it was Barnabas who first introduced Saul to the apostles in Jerusalem (Acts 9:27). The same was true in Antioch, where Barnabas had established himself as an effective leader after being sent by the apostles. It was not until after he got settled in Antioch that Barnabas recruited Saul to the team. And now, in Paphos, Saul was beginning to assert himself, and Barnabas showed no signs of interfering.

Saul also began to reveal his God-given agenda to intentionally reach out to Gentiles beyond the boundaries of the synagogue. He made a conscious decision to start using his Greek name, Paul, as opposed to his Hebrew name, Saul. It is as though Paul is now proactively positioning himself to pursue the destiny to which God had appointed him, as a "chosen instrument" for the Gentiles (Acts 9:15).

All these changes seem to have been more than John Mark bargained for. When they left Paphos, Paul was clearly in charge. Luke writes, "Paul and his companions sailed to Perga in Pamphylia ..." (Acts 13:13). Barnabas was now listed as an unnamed companion— not of Saul, the Pharisee turned follower of Jesus, but of Paul, the apostle to the Gentiles. Amidst this sea of change, "John left them to return to Jerusalem" (Acts 13:13). In his mind, John may have just been returning home. But in Paul's mind, he was deserting[71] the team (Acts 15:38).

How Values Impact Judgment

Judgment swings on the values of a leader as much as it does the quality of the information available. Paul and Barnabas had the same information from their shared experience of John Mark's internship. But Paul and Barnabas were different leaders.

The birth name of Barnabas was Joseph. The apostles gave him the name Barnabas, which means *son of encouragement,* after he demonstrated generosity by selling a field and donating the money to fund the mission of the early Church. Barnabas was "king of the second chance." When others rejected Saul in Jerusalem, Barnabas met with him. Barnabas also took a considerable risk by giving Saul access to the apostles and, later, by recruiting him to assist with the work in Antioch.

Barnabas placed a high value on people development and was prepared to extend grace, especially to a close relative like John Mark. Paul was equally committed to developing young leaders. One of the very first stops on his second missionary journey was Lystra, where Paul recruited another young leader, Timothy, who would become his "son in the faith" (Acts 16:1–3). But Paul's value system, at least at the time, did not offer the same amount of grace for a second chance with John Mark.

Almost all leaders would affirm the importance of values as the central component of a philosophy of leadership and ministry. Few leaders have explicitly identified their values and developed an understanding of how they impact every judgment call.

How Feedback Informs Judgment

Input from wise counselors is another critical aspect of the judgment framework for hearing the voice of God. Beyond the quality of our information and the clarity of our values, good judgment calls also depend on our ability to receive feedback.

Barnabas no doubt gave Paul feedback on the situation with John Mark, and vice versa. We don't have any record of what was said, nor the spirit in which it was said. But we know Barnabas and Paul were unable to resolve their sharp disagreement and their working relationship. Barnabas embarked on a second missionary journey of his own, with John Mark, but he sailed out of the pages of Scripture in Acts 15, never to be mentioned again.

Whatever issues Paul had with John Mark, they were resolved over time, likely because of input from Barnabas. By the time of Paul's imprisonment in Rome, Mark had become one of his "fellow workers" (Philem. 24). Paul commended Mark to the church at Colossae and instructed believers there, "If he comes to you, welcome him" (Col. 4:10). As Paul's ministry came to a close, he asked Timothy to bring Mark to visit because Mark had been helpful in ministry (2 Tim. 4:11). What changed? Paul's values? John Mark's reliability? Perhaps both.

Feedback is essential to every leader's self-awareness journey. Much of the information associated with decision-making comes in the form of feedback. Therefore, leaders who can't receive feedback well will compromise their ability to make good judgment calls.

In their excellent book, *Thanks for the Feedback*, Douglas Stone and Sheila Heen explain how blind spots limit our ability to receive feedback well. Blind spots are filters that limit our ability to see what other people see and in turn hinder our behavior and our ability to interpret information. Blind spots were very likely a key element of the sharp disagreement between Barnabas and Paul.

Stone and Heen emphasize the process of turning "raw data,"— based on what we observe ourselves and receive from other sources— into advice, decisions, or consequences. We must interpret and label before we make judgments that drive our actions. Paul looked at the same data as Barnabas, but through different filters, and labeled John Mark a deserter.

Like Paul and Barnabas, we interpret our actions and the actions of others with filters that favor our individual understanding of our thoughts, feelings, and motives. We know what we meant to say, not just what we said. We know what we meant to do, even more than what we actually did. Apart from watching ourselves on a reality TV show, we can't see our own actions for what they are. Our blind spots put us at a significant disadvantage when it comes to understanding how others perceive us, until they give us feedback.

The people around us rarely have a full understanding of the thoughts, feelings, and motives behind our words and actions. Even our closest relationships experience conflict because of the gap between what we meant to say or do and how it was interpreted. Their feedback reflects their observation of our behavior, how it impacted them, and the story they are developing based on their interaction with us. All of this is outside of our view and only made visible by feedback.

We don't know if John Mark was given the opportunity to make his case directly to Paul to explain why he left for home on the first missionary journey and why he deserved a second chance. We can only assume that if John Mark tried to make a case, Paul wasn't convinced. Judgment is complicated. And even wise, godly, experienced leaders can get it wrong. In this case, I'll let you decide if it was Paul or Barnabas who got it wrong. Maybe we are left wondering to keep us humble and prayerful as we apply the judgment framework to our decisions.

How Judgment Calls Become Pivot Points

I began this chapter by asserting that the legacy of leaders, and the success of the organizations they lead, will be determined by the cumulative outcome of their most important judgment calls. These decisions often become pivot points.

Leadership Emergence Theory, which I first mentioned in the opening chapter, defines a pivot point as a critical time of God's dealing with a leader, the outcome of which hinges on how we respond to the life-shaping experiences God allows. Our pivot points have a disproportionate influence on the trajectory of our leadership journey. Bad judgment in a pivot-point moment can curtail future leadership potential and opportunity. Really bad judgment can shut down a leader's future completely, as with disqualifying failures examined in chapter four.

We have no control over when we will be called upon to make high-stakes judgments that may set the course of a lifetime for the people and organizations we serve, and thereby write the most influential chapters of our leadership biography. Yet we do control the priority we give and the effort we expend to identify our values, expose our blind spots, and tune our prayerful attention to hearing the voice of God. At the pivot points of your leadership journey, when you need to exercise sound judgment, you won't have time to prepare. It will be too late to engage deeply in the Bible or build a trusted network of wise counselors.

Perhaps the most strategic judgment call every leader can make is to seriously approach preparation for making wise decisions. No wonder the wisest man to ever live said: "Wisdom is supreme; therefore get wisdom. Though it cost you all you have, get understanding" (Prov. 4:7). The question isn't whether we will be asked to make hard calls as leaders, but whether we will be ready.

CHAPTER 11

Becoming a
Bible-Centered Leader

Becoming a Bible-Centered Leader

Executive Summary

It is possible to know a lot about the Bible and a lot about leadership without being a Bible-centered leader. Not all leaders have the spiritual gift of leadership. All leaders do have at least one "word" gift. The number and type of a leader's word gifts shapes the Bible-engagement strategy. Word-gifted leaders utilize the Equipping Formula: devotional input, in-depth study, familiarity reading, and topical study. In-depth study focuses on biblical content God has used to spur a leader's growth. In-depth study calls for a different set of study skills, based on the type of biblical content.

"If you have read the entire Bible, every verse on every page, stand up," the conference speaker said to a room packed with college students. I didn't move. Nobody else did either. Though it happened many years ago, this moment remains vivid in my memory.

A combination of awkwardness and uncertainty filled the air. But the speaker was quick to erase our doubts. He began repeating his question with even more enthusiasm, encouraging anyone who could confidently answer *yes* to stand up.

I wanted to stand.

I think I've read the entire Bible. I must have. I'm a Bible college student. Of course I have!

Then in a moment of honest reflection I admitted to myself that if I had read the entire Bible, it was by accident, not on purpose. And this speaker called for a level of confidence I knew I didn't have.

His larger-than-life personality wasn't just for showmanship, though he had a great flair for it. He wore a jacket covered with a map of the world and held a giant inflatable globe over his head for emphasis during his talk. He left no room for doubt about his passion for the world and the Word of God.

Maybe you've heard of him—George Verwer, the founder and former international director of Operation Mobilization, which has spread the gospel in eighty-five countries.

George exhorted us to remember that if we were to serve in missions or ministry, the Bible would be, and must be, our primary resource. We couldn't expect to deepen our personal faith or help others do the same without a growing understanding of the Bible.

I felt guilty that I hadn't read the entire Bible. But George went on to provide a strategy, fulfilling one of my favorite Verwerisms: "The only thing wrong with a guilt trip is if you get sent there on a one-way ticket." He had no intention of sending a roomful of students to a futile destination. Just the opposite, he gave us a return ticket that could take us into the heart of God's Word.

George explained a plan to divide the Bible into its natural sections with three-by-five cards as bookmarks for the Pentateuch, Historical Books, Wisdom Literature, Prophetic Books, Gospels and Acts, and the Epistles. He challenged us to read one chapter in each section every day. The cards served not only as bookmarks, but also as places to record verses we would memorize or explore through further study. In addition, he recommended reading *What the Bible Is All About* by Henrietta Mears, which gave an overview of each book in the Bible and helped answer big-picture questions we might encounter along the way.

I took up his challenge immediately with a promise to myself that I would read the Bible—every verse on every page—within the following year. And so began an adventure of Bible engagement that transformed my life.

Later, I would discover these words from George Müller, whose Bible reading habits had informed the daily system George Verwer passed along:

> But it pleased God, through the instrumentality of a beloved Christian brother, to rouse in me an earnestness about the Word, and ever since then I have been a lover of it.
>
> Let me press upon you my first point, that of attending regularly to reading through the Scriptures.... Why is this so deeply important? Simply that we may see the connection between one book and another of the Bible, and between one chapter and another.
>
> And this will be of particular advantage to us, in case we should become laborers in Christ's vineyard; because in expounding the Word, we shall be able to refer to every part of it.... I have, as I said before, known the blessedness of this plan for forty-six years, and though I am now nearly seventy years of age, and though I have been converted for nearly fifty years, I can say, by the grace of God, that I more than ever love the Word of God, and have greater delight than ever in reading it.
>
> And though I have read the Word nearly a hundred times right through, I have never got tired of reading it, and this more especially through reading it regularly, consecutively, day by day, and not merely reading a chapter here or there, as my own thoughts might have led me to do.[72]

George Verwer did for me what an unnamed Christian brother did for George Müller. He roused in me an earnestness about the Word, and ever since then I have been a lover of it.

What Is a Bible-Centered Leader?

In the opening chapter to this book I explained my goal—beyond highlighting the findings of my research—to stimulate your passion to engage the Bible as a primary source for leadership insight. I sought to convince you how rich the Bible is with leadership gold. Then in chapters one through ten, I revealed some of those riches from my personal study.

In this final chapter, I want to take you inside the instruction manual that will help you dig deeper, using your spiritual drill rig to unearth valuable treasures of your own. Instruction manuals read differently from narrative chapters, so you will notice the change of pace and flow on the following pages. The biggest payoff from an instruction manual isn't just reading it through in one pass and setting it aside. As you drill down, come back to this manual to revisit specific details. You will probably want to return to it more than once as you build your own Bible-centered leadership development plan.

BibleCenteredLeadership.com

In the resource section of BibleCenteredLeadership.com you will find an online Bible-Centered Leadership Development Planner to guide your step-by-step process of applying information in this chapter to your own journey.

Just as God used George Verwer, and the daily reading system of George Müller, to rouse my earnestness about reading the Bible, God also used Bobby Clinton to help me engage the Bible as a primary source for leadership. Bobby defines a Bible-centered leader as:

> One whose leadership is informed by the Bible, and who has been personally shaped by biblical leadership values, who has grasped the intent of Scriptural books and their content in such a way as to apply them to current situations and who uses the Bible in ministry so as to impact followers.[73]

It is possible to know a lot about the Bible and a lot about leadership without being a Bible-centered leader. Remember the opening chapter's real-life picture of Bible-centered leadership through the words of Samuel Logan Brengle? You may want to turn back to those words to refresh your vision of what it looks like to become best friends with leaders in the Bible who help you fall more deeply in love with Jesus.

My favorite example of Bible-centered leadership in Scripture is Ezra. He led during the Transitional Leadership Era to bring a group of exiles from Babylon back to Jerusalem. Zerubbabel had pioneered the return before Ezra, and Nehemiah would come after him. Ezra played a meaningful support role for Nehemiah after he arrived and began rebuilding the walls of the city.

On one occasion, after the walls of Jerusalem had been rebuilt, Ezra led a national assembly. He stood on a high wooden platform built specifically for this gathering and read from the Law of Moses. A group of Levites assisted Ezra: "They read from the Book of the Law of God, making it clear and giving the meaning so that the people could understand what was being read" (Neh. 8:8).

The favor of God was on Ezra's life and ministry, emphasized repeatedly by the phrase, "the hand of his God was on him" (Ezra 7:9). The defining verse about Ezra's leadership that helps explain God's favor on his life says: "For Ezra had devoted himself to the study and observance of the Law of the LORD, and to teaching its decrees and laws in Israel" (Ezra 7:10).

In the original Hebrew, *devoted* literally means he *set his heart firmly*. We find the same idea conveyed in the words of King Hezekiah, who prayed for the people, "May the LORD, who is good, pardon everyone who sets his heart on seeking God" (2 Chron. 30:18–19).

Bible-centered leadership begins with a commitment of the heart to seek after God by engaging his Word. The Holy Spirit invited me to devote myself to this journey through the example of George Müller and the challenge of George Verwer. I took deeper steps, when I encountered the teaching of Bobby Clinton, as I explain in detail on the pages to come.

What about you? Have you devoted yourself, like Ezra or Müller or Verwer or Brengle? Reading this book is likely a sign that you are at least open to the idea of more intentional engagement with the Bible as a primary source for your leadership. But using the Bible as a ministry tool is different from being personally shaped by biblical leadership values. I hope to rouse you to a new level of earnestness about both, but especially the latter.

Bible-centered leadership is not a sexy topic for ministry leaders today. Research done by Barna Group for the American Bible Society confirms widespread skepticism about the authority of the Bible:

> For a sizable number who start out as Christians, waning trust in God's Word is where they begin

to lose their religion. Yes, the vast majority of American households owns a Bible, and millions of people, even non-Christians, revere what they know (or have heard) about its wisdom. Yet through research for the American Bible Society, we have tracked an increasing percentage of Americans who say the Bible is just another book written by men, not the inspired Word of God.

When the Bible goes, so goes good faith. This is a huge threat among the next generation.

Among Elders in the United States (age seventy and older), three out of four believe the Bible to be authoritative, and the ratio of those who are engaged with the Bible to those who are skeptical is 4:1. Among the youngest generation of Americans (Millennials, age eighteen to thirty-one), fewer than half believe the Bible is authoritative, and the ratio of Bible engagement to skepticism is 1:2.... Millennial non-Christians are much more likely than older Americans to view the Bible as "just a story" (50 percent), "mythology" (38 percent), or "a fairy tale" (30 percent).[74]

The data on Gen Z is equally disturbing, as this cohort is growing up to follow in the footsteps of its Gen X parents, who increasingly have no religious affiliation. According to James Emery White, many in Gen Z have no memory of the gospel.[75] Cultural forces play a part in the backstory on this data. But what if the skepticism about the authority of the Bible is also a result of the lack of Bible-centered leaders?

Perhaps the best remedy to arrest this diminishing view of the Bible is a groundswell of leaders whose lives are shaped by biblical leadership values? What if your personal journey, as well as that of the leaders you develop and the followers you influence, could be part of a movement that helps stem this tide?

Ezra set his heart firmly to study, obey, and teach the law of God. This threefold commitment motivates me every time I reflect on it. Knowledge by itself is not a mark of maturity. It must be matched by obedience. Leaders who understand the Bible and apply it to current situations gain authority to teach it to others, making its meaning clear, so that the people can understand what is being read (Neh. 8:8).

Leadership, Word Giftedness, and Bible Engagement

The journey to becoming a Bible-centered leader isn't the same for everyone because spiritual gifts vary and, accordingly, so do approaches to Bible engagement. When you understand the variations, you can more intentionally cultivate leadership capacity in yourself and others.

Leadership Emergence Theory advocates that effective leaders view leadership selection and development as a priority function. Therefore, one of the most important responsibilities of every leader is to recruit and develop other leaders. Why? Because, God's primary means for releasing His blessing to followers is through leaders.[76] When we fail to develop leaders in our ministry, we limit the outpouring of God's blessing to followers.

The simplest illustration of this reality is the small groups ministry of a local church. The bottleneck for establishing groups is almost always a lack of leaders. Failure to develop more leaders restricts the blessing God wants to pour out as groups experience life in community.

A second observation, from thousands of Leadership Emergence Theory case studies,[77] is that all leaders have at least one word gift in their spiritual-gift mix, but not necessarily the gift of leadership. It may seem counterintuitive that a leader would not have the spiritual gift of leadership because special functions associated with inciting others toward vision are best done by leaders with that gift. But even without it, leaders can gain influence with followers through other spiritual gifts. What all leaders do have in common is the presence of at least one word gift.

The number and type of word gifts entrusted by the Holy Spirit to a leader plays a critical role in shaping that leader's Bible-engagement strategy. To put it another way, the journey toward Bible-centered leadership will look different from one leader to another, based on the type of word gifts each one possesses.[78]

Since the idea of word gifts may be new to you, I want to explain it in context by summarizing the corporate functions of spiritual gifts.

The Corporate Functions of Spiritual Gifts

One way to categorize the corporate functions of spiritual gifts in a community of believers is to recognize three clusters: *power gifts, love gifts,* and *word gifts.*[79] Some spiritual gifts function in only one cluster, while others can function in more than one, such as both power and love, or power and word.

Power gifts provide authenticity and credibility. They confirm the reality of the unseen God.

Love gifts demonstrate the beauty of God's work in our lives and the practical expression of our relationship with him. They help the world see and experience God's love in action.

Word gifts help people know God's character and purposes, what he expects from us, and how we can join in his work. Word-gifted leaders communicate about and for God.

All the spiritual gifts are important. Some are called for more directly, based on what is needed in the moment. When functioning together in a body of believers, all three gift clusters provide a well-rounded testimony about God and his work in our lives.

The cluster of word gifts holds special importance for leadership development because all leaders have at least one word gift. The presence of word gifts provides important evidence of leadership potential to be nurtured. Leaders who effectively develop other spiritual leaders actively refine their ability to see the potential of word giftedness. Emerging leaders typically begin using word gifts before they explicitly identify them. Helping young leaders identify the presence of word gifts enables them to develop their gifts on purpose and use them with more authority. The type of word gifts present is important for framing the pathway toward Bible-centered leadership.

Corporate Functions of Spiritual Gifts

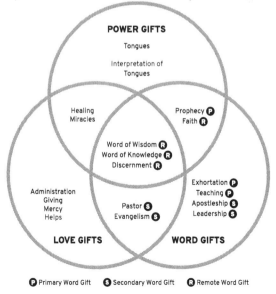

POWER GIFTS

Tongues

Interpretation of Tongues

Healing
Miracles

Prophecy **P**
Faith **R**

Word of Wisdom **R**
Word of Knowledge **R**
Discernment **R**

Exhortation **P**
Teaching **P**
Apostleship **S**
Leadership **S**

Administration
Giving
Mercy
Helps

Pastor **S**
Evangelism **S**

LOVE GIFTS   **WORD GIFTS**

P Primary Word Gift   **S** Secondary Word Gift   **R** Remote Word Gift

Three Levels of Word Gifts

All word gifts call for the use of the Bible in ministry. Some word gifts call for more direct engagement with God's Word than others. Because this concept is so critical to Bible-centered leadership, I quote Bobby Clinton directly:

> I believe there are various levels of word gifts in regard to the importance of knowing the Bible, studying the Bible and using the Bible in ministry. Every leader who operates in a word gift needs to be at least familiar with the Bible. It is a leader's primary source and ultimate authority of revelation about who God is and what he expects. However, in my opinion, leaders operating in certain word gifts need to be grounded more thoroughly than other leaders operating in other word gifts. I have thus broken up the word gifts into three levels ...in terms of how grounded they must be in the Word.[80]

The three levels of word gifts are primary, secondary, and remote.[81]

Primary Word Gifts
The three primary word gifts are teaching, exhortation, and prophecy. They enable members of the body of Christ to explain who God is and what he desires from us. Teachers clarify new truth. Exhorters help us apply truth to daily life. Listeners often respond to the gift of teaching by saying, *I never saw that before!* Listeners often respond to the gift of exhortation by saying, *That is so practical! I have to apply that to my life today.*

Prophets provide correction or perspective on a specific situation. We often respond to prophets with the recognition their words are good medicine but hard to swallow. To operate with primary word gifts, leaders require deep knowledge of God and His ways as revealed in Scripture. The fruitful exercise of these gifts calls for a strong understanding of the Bible and requires disciplined engagement over a lifetime to be effective.

Secondary Word Gifts
The four secondary word gifts are leadership, apostleship, evangelism, and pastoring. They do not primarily clarify who God is but rather use his Word to accomplish other important functions in the body of Christ. Leaders with the spiritual gift of leadership incite

others toward vision. Evangelists introduce other people to the gospel. Pastors care for the growth and development of followers. Those with the gift of apostleship create new ministry structures.

Remote Word Gifts
The four remote word gifts are discernment, faith, word of knowledge, and word of wisdom. Remote word gifts call for a primary dependency on the ministry of the Holy Spirit as opposed to an accumulated body of biblical knowledge. These gifts will never contradict the written Word, but because they focus on the immediate setting, they bring a topical word from God.

Bobby Clinton has identified several implications flowing from the three levels of word gifting. They are brief but essential and worthy of including here.[82]

- All leaders are word gifted and need the equipping that only can come from the Bible. Therefore, all Jesus-following leaders need a basic familiarity with the Bible.
- Beyond basic familiarity, not all leaders need to be grounded in the Bible at the same level. Leaders with primary word gifts must go deeper than those with secondary or remote word gifts.
- Bible study disciplines and goals will be different for leaders at each level of word giftedness. Leaders with primary word gifts require more aggressive growth habits than others.
- Leaders with secondary and remote word gifts can expect an interdependent relationship with leaders who have primary word gifts. People without word gifts seek the same interdependence.
- Almost all leaders are multi-gifted and will at times experience overlap among the three levels of word gifting. But an individual's gift mix usually has a dominant gift, which will typically indicate the level of word giftedness.

In summary, your level of word giftedness will play a critical role in shaping how you engage the Bible and continue your journey toward Bible-centered leadership.

An Equipping Formula for Bible-Centered Leadership Development

Based on your word gifts—and the word gifts you recognize in emerging leaders—you can take an intentional approach to Bible-centered leadership development, using what Bobby Clinton calls the *Equipping Formula*. This formula offers a strategic way for word-gifted leaders to engage in Bible study as a lifelong journey. The Equipping Formula includes the following four components.

Equipping Formula

| DEVOTIONAL INPUT | IN-DEPTH STUDY | TOPICAL STUDY | FAMILIARITY READING | LIFELONG BIBLE MASTERY |

Let's take a closer look at the Equipping Formula and how leaders relate to the Bible through each component.

Devotional Input

We pursue intimacy with God, using the Bible to feed our soul and shape our character. This kind of spiritual input is a primary means by which all believers, especially leaders, get to know God better and keep their own well full.

In-Depth Study

We engage in ongoing and in-depth study of different Bible books, characters, passages or topics God has used mightily to spur our growth, solve our problems, or otherwise meet our needs. As we study our core biblical material, God reveals more of himself and his redemptive purposes. This material is or will become our favorite Scripture, which we will use again and again in our ministry.

An individual cannot master the entire Bible, nor should they try to do so. But each person can lean on the greater understanding within the body of Christ. Each person can move toward mastery in the knowledge of specific Bible books, passages, and characters and the important lessons they teach. A leader will then become adept at applying these lessons in any setting to powerfully impact followers. The amount of in-depth study a leader will pursue over a lifetime is a function of their level of word giftedness.

Familiarity Reading

While we will not be able to do in-depth study of the whole Bible, we can become generally familiar with every part of God's Word. We accomplish this mainly through the disciplined and systematic reading of the whole Bible, over time. If you have never done so, it would be advisable to include a purposeful reading of the whole Bible in your spiritual training program, in addition to whatever you are doing for devotional input. My experience in working with emerging leaders who have primary word gifts suggests that reading the Bible cover-to-cover at least five times over a number of years is required to establish a solid base of familiarity.

Topical Study

We study specific passages or topics when our interest is piqued by way of familiarity reading or devotional input. Topical study may also arise from being asked to speak to a group on a specific theme in a variety of settings.

The first two components of the Equipping Formula—devotional input and in-depth study—should be an ongoing part of every leader's spiritual training program. The last two components can be included intermittently as needed.

In-Depth Study of Your Personal Core Material

Bobby Clinton identified a breakthrough insight for Bible-centered leadership in the idea that each leader can uniquely discover and develop *core material* in the Bible. He explains:

> Leaders usually have favorite Bible books, or special passages, which God has used mightily in their own lives to spur their growth or solve their problems or otherwise meet them. It is these books or special passages which form the basis for much of what they share with others in their ministry. And they usually do so with added impact since these core items have meant something to them personally.[83]

The focus of a leader's in-depth study should be to move toward mastery of the books, characters, passages, themes, and other impactful content such as Psalms or parables. Each type of core material will call for a different set of Bible study skills, which will need to be developed along the way. You can find resources developed by Bobby Clinton, step-by-step study outlines, and sample material at BibleCenteredLeadership.com. We will continue to add resources to this website to serve a growing movement of Bible-centered leaders.

Leaders with primary word gifts should expect to have more core material than those with secondary word gifts. And similarly, leaders with secondary word gifts will have more core material than those with remote word gifts.

Clearly, the idea of core material is extrabiblical and was

developed from interaction with Jesus-following leaders studying Leadership Emergence Theory. But I've personally tested this idea, as has Bobby, with hundreds of leaders who, after modest reflection, can identify the primary components of their core material. I've helped many leaders get started with this process. Here are a few pointers to consider.

Identifying Your Core Material for In-Depth Study

Keep in mind this process is more of an art than a science, and it is built on your subjective or intuitive processing of key factors. The amount of core material you will have and be able to identify is a function of three variables:

- Level of word giftedness
- Current Bible knowledge
- Age and experience

If there are parts of the Bible you haven't engaged, you may be like me at the missions conference I described at the start of this chapter, having yet to discover the core material that provides a foundation for Bible-centered leadership. That's why your current level of Bible knowledge is an important factor. You may want to consider taking a basic Bible knowledge test to get a better idea where you stand. Go to BibleCenteredLeadership.com for information about free Bible tests.

Age and experience are important factors as well. We can expect God to meet us at various times in our life with specific revelation from his Word that is exactly what we need in the moment. We can't force this. It only happens over time. We just need to be wise enough to look for direction in the Bible and to be receptive to the Holy Spirit as we read.

The following steps have proven helpful to others on this journey:

1. Make a list of your favorite books and characters in the Bible—the ones you have been drawn to, repeatedly read about, or in which God has met you in a specific or meaningful way.

2. Add to your list any book or character you have always wanted to study, but you have not accomplished it yet. If you are confident of your gift mix, have a reasonable familiarity

with the Bible, and at least five years of ministry experience, you shouldn't have too much difficulty with this process.

3. If you are unsure of your gift mix, have not read through the Bible at least once, and have less than five years of ministry experience, don't try to make a full list. Just pick one core book and one core character for in-depth study now. Make it a priority to refine your understanding of your spiritual gifts. Increase your overall familiarity with the Bible by following a reading plan, such as the one I explained at the beginning of this chapter.

Designing Your Bible-Centered Leadership Development Plan

I realize this chapter may seem a bit overwhelming, especially if you are not currently engaged in a carefully designed plan to study the Bible. Don't allow the feeling of being overwhelmed to keep you from getting started. Here are a few practical guidelines that can help you reduce any anxious feelings.

Plan Ahead

Plan your interaction with the Bible six months or a year at a time, using the Equipping Formula as your template. Most organizational leaders look that far ahead when designing a marketing or strategic plan. It is common to design personal growth goals a year at a time. Most pastors plan that far ahead when it comes to a preaching schedule. There isn't any reason you can't do the same when it comes to applying the Equipping Formula to your Bible-centered leadership development plan.

Overlap Intentionally

Overlap your devotional input with your in-depth study projects whenever possible. From my experience, this is the single most important insight that will affect your ability to follow through. You won't have time to engage the Bible devotionally and do in-depth study of your core material separately. Don't try. Learn how to integrate the devotional aspect with your in-depth study. If you are studying a book, character, passage, or other core element, invite God to speak to you and spend time actively listening. Don't turn this into an academic task that sucks all the mystery and wonder out of the process.

Strengthen Your Bible Knowledge

Select your familiarity reading to strengthen your overall Bible knowledge. Once you have read the whole Bible through at least one time, plan your familiarity reading based on the sections of the Bible where your knowledge is the weakest. This is where a Bible test can help, by showing you the sections of the Scripture you need to study the most.

Avoid Comparison

Be careful not to project your approach to Bible study on others who do not have the same level of word giftedness as you have. The more you embrace the Equipping Formula and the appropriate level of in-depth study for your word giftedness, the more tempted you will be to compare your approach to others and impose your plan on them, regardless of what spiritual gifts they have.

I made this mistake for years, challenging people to embrace a level of study that wasn't appropriate for their level of giftedness. When I learned about this danger, I felt like I needed to go on an apology tour to ask forgiveness from the people I'd sent on a guilt trip with a one-way ticket.

What Are You Going to Be?

With the tools in this chapter, you can join and encourage a journey of Bible-centered leadership, in the company of "prophets and priests, and kings" ... and in "communion with apostles, saints, and martyrs, and with Jesus." I began this book with these inspirational words of Samuel Logan Brengle. And I reminded you the odds are stacked against us when it comes to finishing well. There is no shortcut to this level of Bible engagement or spiritual intimacy.

I want to close with two lessons from the life of another Bible-centered leader, G. Campbell Morgan, flowing from pivotal moments in his journey.

G. Campbell Morgan grew up in the home of a Christian minister and was preaching by the time he was in middle school. Through his high school years, Morgan didn't think "there could be any honest and respectable man who could doubt that the Bible was the Word of God." But at the turn of the twentieth century, the physical sciences were exploding with the discovery of new ways to understand the world. Gradually, scientific discovery eclipsed his faith. He later said, "When the sun is eclipsed the light is not killed, it is hidden. There came a moment when I was sure of nothing."[84]

Morgan, at age nineteen, canceled all his preaching appointments.

His biography, drawing from his family records, tells the story of his turnaround:

> Then, taking all his books, both those attacking and those defending the Bible, he put them all in a corner cupboard.... He went out of the house, and down the street to a bookshop. He bought a new Bible, and returning to his room with it, he said to himself: 'I am no longer sure that this is what my father claims it to be—the Word of God. But of this I *am* sure. If it *be* the Word of God, and if I come to it with an unprejudiced and open mind, it will bring assurance to my soul of itself.' ... "That Bible *found* me," he said, "I began to read and study it then, in 1883. I have been a student ever since, and still am."[85]

Morgan said those words—"that Bible found me"—in 1938, fifty-five years after he emerged from his eclipse of faith, totally convinced the Bible is true and nothing but the living Word of God. This reality birthed in Morgan a conviction, like Ezra's, to study, obey, and teach the Bible.

Not every Bible-centered leader experiences a crisis of faith. But every Bible-centered leader can come to own the same conviction as Morgan, that the Bible is the authoritative Word of God. It doesn't have to be defended. It can convince people if it is clearly taught and if people sense a need to which the truth in the Bible speaks.[86]

In his late twenties, Morgan served as a pastor at Rugeley, England. An effective communicator, he found many opportunities to speak inside and outside the local church. His public recognition increased as his giftedness and Bible knowledge became evident. One Sunday evening, after Morgan preached at his church, several people walked forward to the altar to receive Christ. God stirred in Morgan's heart a question that pressed his conscience.

> I went home to my own study, and sat there alone. As clearly as though it had sounded in the room, a voice put this question, 'What are you going to be, a preacher, or My messenger?' For a moment I knew not what it meant, except to realize that the Spirit of God had created a crisis. I stood at the parting of the ways. Presently I began to ponder that night's sermon—to review my ministry. To my dismay I discovered that the desire to become, and to be

known as a great preacher, was beginning to get the upper hand.[87]

Morgan sat in his study reflecting on this question all night. Just before dawn he sealed the answer—to be God's messenger—by taking years of sermons, infused with too much of "self," and tossing them in the fire. That moment became a pivot point. Watching the papers burn, Morgan cried out to God, committing to speak only what God gave him— adding nothing, taking nothing away.

Regardless of our platform for influence, or level of giftedness, we all have to answer the question: What are you going to be, a speaker or God's messenger? Morgan was a powerful communicator. If your word gifts are buttressed by strengths and acquired skills that make you effective on stage, you can expect to be tempted to lean on raw talent instead of a deep knowledge of God's Word. Communication skills can produce in-the-moment responses that feed the ego. But only the power and truth of God's Word can produce life change that lasts.

I'm asking God to help me become his messenger, and it inspires me to pursue a lifelong journey toward Bible-centered leadership.

I hope I've inspired you to join me.

Chapter 00

[1] Hall, Clarence. *Samuel Logan Brengle: Portrait of a Prophet*, Salvation Army, 1933, 182–183.

[2] Ibid, 247–248.

[3] Ibid, 183.

[4] Ibid, 63.

[5] Bobby has six Eras: Patriarchal, Pre-kingdom, Kingdom, Post-Kingdom, Pre-Church, Church.

[6] It is impossible to overstate the influence Bobby Clinton had on me in developing this process. This entire framework and these specific questions flow from what I learned, studying under Bobby with his continued engagement as my primary leadership mentor.

[7] Bobby Clinton refers to Hebrews 13:7 as the leadership mandate.

Chapter 01

[8] http://articles.latimes.com/1997–06–07/local/me-1034_1_billy-graham-recalls.

[9] Robert, Dana. *Occupy Until I Come*, 2003. Wm. B. Eerdmans Publishing Co., 144.

[10] Ibid, 45.

[11] Ibid, 45.

[12] Ibid, 148.

[13] Murray, Andrew. *Humility, HeavenReigns*.com., 18.

[14] Ibid, 18.

[15] I am building on ideas developed by Andrew Murray in his book, *Humility*, 18.

Chapter 02

[16] The leadership structure described in Numbers 16, was already in place at the time the spies were sent out in Numbers 13. The leadership conversation in Numbers 16 is fascinating, with 250 "well-known community leaders who had been appointed members of the council" coming as a group to oppose Moses. It sheds light on the complexity of the various leadership structures in place, some of which may have carried over from the internal organization of the Israelites in Egypt.

[17] This definition of self-awareness is modified from Daniel Goleman's writing about emotional intelligence.

[18] I have developed a self-leadership resource called the Identity Profile Self-Awareness Tool (IPSAT), which is being used by individuals, as well as in churches, organizations and universities, to help people understand the unique combination of personality, strengths, skills, spiritual gifts, and passions. For more information visit myIPSAT.com.

[19] I had the privilege of leading EFMA through a rebrand, becoming The Mission Exchange, and then a merger, to become what is now Missio Nexus. I transitioned out of that role to launch nexleader in 2015.

[20] Leadership Filtration Theory was pioneered by Harvard Professor Gautam Mukunda, in his book, *Indispensable: When Leaders Really Matter.*

[21] In Leadership Emergence Theory this is called the response premise.

[22] Remember, this is no longer just the ten spies making a case to return to Egypt. The whole assembly, according to Numbers 14:2, presented this to Moses. The "whole assembly" is not referring to all one million Israelites, it is a representative group of top leaders.

[23] This is based on the widely referenced research of Dr. J. Robert Clinton. See *Leadership Perspectives*, Barnabas Resources, 93–98.

[24] Ibid.

Chapter 03

[25] This is a macro leadership principle identified by Bobby Clinton.

[26] Convergence is a Leadership Emergence Theory concept that reflects the ideal interaction of giftedness and influence with opportunity and role. It is the result of living a focused life over time.

[27] Moving back to Ramah at about age seventeen means Samuel was likely reunited with his mother, who had taken him to Shiloh as a boy.

[28] This principle is a key finding in Leadership Emergence Theory and one of seven major leadership lessons evidenced in effective leadership. It is referenced repeatedly by J. Robert Clinton in his writings.

[29] This comes from the excellent book, *Buy In*, by John Kotter and Lorne Whitehead.

Chapter 04

[30] Pellerin, Charles. *How NASA Builds Teams*, 6 Published by John Wiley and Sons.

[31] My thinking about failure has been influenced strongly by Dr. J. Robert Clinton's Leadership Emergence Theory related to pivot points, and Tom Marshall's book, *Understanding Leadership*, 212–215, published by Sovereign World, 1991.

[32] The character and competency of a leader overlap in the implementation of leadership influence. I categorize Rehoboam's failure as competency-based because it was fundamentally a poor judgment, relying on bad advice. We don't know enough about what was in Rehoboam's heart to say with confidence his attempt to solidify his influence in the eyes of the people was based on flawed character. We can say with confidence it was bad leadership.

[33] I am not suggesting it is unbiblical to terminate a person for lack of competency. Being removed from a job or role by a supervising boss is not the same as being disqualified by God.

Chapter 05

[34] This is how Bobby Clinton defines a leader in *Leadership Emergence Theory*.

[35] Jacob had twelve sons, which became the twelve tribes of Israel. But the descendants of Levi served as priests and were not given an inheritance of land. Joseph's two sons, Ephraim and Manasseh, though from the same tribe, were given an inheritance of

the land.

[36] This is a macro leadership principle identified by Bobby Clinton, in his book, *The Bible and Leadership Values.*

[37] This is a macro leadership principle identified by Bobby Clinton, in his book, *The Bible and Leadership Values.*

Chapter 06

[38] Piper, John. *Let The Nations Be Glad: The Supremacy of God in Missions,* 1993. Baker Books, 11.

[39] Ibid, 26.

[40] Tozer, A.W. *The Knowledge of the Holy,* 1961, Harper & Row, 5.

[41] Dorsett, Lyle W. *A Passion For Souls,* 1997, Moody Press, 20

[42] A slightly modified version of the opening sentence from *The Knowledge of the Holy,* AW Tozer, Harper & Row, 1961, 4.

[43] Tozer, A.W. Compiled by Gerald B. Smith, *What Ever Happened to Worship,* 1985, compiled by Gerald B. Smith, Christian Publications, 31.

[44] Daniel is not mentioned in chapter three at all. We can be sure he wasn't among those who bowed to the statue. So the only other logical explanation is his special status exempted him from this meeting. His three Hebrew friends were serving in an administrative role and were required to be present for the unveiling of the statue.

[45] Nebuchadnezzar clearly recognized the fourth person in the furnace was not human. The text is not definitive, but most scholars believe this was an appearance of the Second Person of the Trinity, Jesus, pre-incarnate.

[46] Dr. Clinton calls this the presence principle, and it is one of the key macro leadership values in the Bible.

Chapter 07

[47] Tozer, A.W. Compiled by Gerald B. Smith, *What Ever Happened to Worship,* 1985, Christian Publications, 20.

[48] Moore, Steve, *Who Is My Neighbor? Being a Good Samaritan in a Connected World,* 2010, 125.

[49] Lewis C.S. *The Lion, the Witch, and the Wardrobe,* Harper Collins, 2000, 80.

[50] Tozer A. W, Worship: The Missing Jewel of the Evangelical Church, 26–27.

[51] http://www.desiringgod.org/articles/a-call-for-christian-risk.

[52] Grubb, Norman. *C. T. Studd Cricketer & Pioneer,* Christian Literature Crusade, 1933, 1982, 120-121.

Chapter 08

[53] This was originally published as part of the introduction to chapter 3 of my book, *Seize the Vuja de,* available online for free at www.SeizeTheVujade.com.

[54] Osborne, Larry. *Accidental Pharisees,* Zondervan, 2012, 24.

[55] Ibid, 18.

56 Willard, Dallas. *The Great Omission*, Kindle location 1485.

57 Ibid, Kindle location 2020.

58 Taylor, William. *Practically Radical*, Kindle location 3457.

59 Marshall, Tom. *Understanding Leadership,* Sovereign World, 83.

60 Tozer, A.W. *The Pursuit of God*, 63–64.

61   http://www.charactercincinnati.org/Faith/Qualities/Meekness/bookertwashinghton.htm.

62 Tozer, A.W. *The Pursuit of Man*, Christian Publications, 214.

Chapter 09

63 I first encountered this framework in a workshop presented by Bruce Wilkinson in 1986.

64 Willard, Dallas. *The Great Omission,* Kindle location, 357.

Chapter 10

65 Wansink, Brian and Jeffrey Sobal (2007), *"Mindless Eating: The 200 Daily Food Decisions We Overlook,"* Environment and Behavior 39:1, 106–123.

66 Tichy, Noel, Bennis, Warren. *Judgment*, Penguin, Kindle location 142.

67 Ibid, Kindle location 400.

68 To the best of my understanding, neither Buck Hatch or Bobby Clinton directly overlaid this framework on Acts 15, but I have found it a helpful way to illustrate the key concepts.

69 The exact time of Peter's visit to Antioch is a topic of debate among scholars. I agree with those who believe it was shortly after the Jerusalem Council.

70 Colossians 4:10 establishes Mark as the relative of Barnabas. Some translations describe them as cousins. The literal translation suggests Mark was Barnabas's sister's son, and is reflected as such in some translations. Commentators differ on how to reconcile this wording. Cousin or nephew, they were close relatives.

71 Luke uses this same original language word in Luke 8:13, in the parable of the sower. Jesus describes the seed that fell among the rocks as people who believe, "but in the time of testing they *fall away.*" (Italics show the same original language word.) It is important to remember that Luke gave us this account based on Paul's report. Luke did not enter the picture until later, during Paul's second missionary journey, so he was dependent upon the record of Paul for information. While it is true that Paul's version, as recorded by Luke, is inspired by the Holy Spirit, it is also only one side of the story. Barnabas is not mentioned again in Acts after chapter 15. It is unlikely that Luke ever heard about these details from Barnabas.

Chapter 11

72 http://www.wholesomewords.org/biography/bmuller15.html.

73 Clinton, J. Robert. *Having Ministry that Lasts*, Barnabas Publishers, 17.

74 Kinnaman, David, Lyons, Gabe. *Good Faith: Being a Christian When Society Thinks You're Irrelevant and Extreme*, Baker Books, 225-226.

[75] White, James, Emery. *Meet Generation Z*, Baker Books, 66.

[76] This is a Macro principle identified by Bobby Clinton as the Blessing Principle.

[77] In my last meeting with Bobby and his son Richard, the number of case studies was approaching 5,000. Bobby's Lifelong Leadership Development course is still being taught in a number of settings, so the data set is increasing.

[78] Everything I have learned about Bible-centered Leadership comes from the teaching of Bobby Clinton, primarily from his textbook, *Having Ministry that Lasts*. It will not be practical to footnote every idea individually. Where direct references are made I will list the source. But for the larger flow of information I offer this umbrella citation, with Bobby's blessing.

[79] Clinton, J. Robert. *Having Ministry that Lasts*, Barnabas Publishers, 21.

[80] Ibid, 58.

[81] Dr. Clinton's labels for these three levels are foundational, superstructural, and remote. I have found primary, and secondary more accessible to groups unfamiliar with his teaching on spiritual gifts.

[82] I've modified Bobby's implications slightly and omitted one for clarity. The list comes from *Having Ministry that Lasts*, 61.

[83] Clinton, J. Robert. *Having Ministry that Lasts*, Barnabas Publishers, 63.

[84] Morgan, Jill. *A Man of the Word*, The G. Campbell Morgan archive, 19.

[85] Ibid, 20.

[86] Clinton, J. Robert. *Having Ministry that Lasts*, Barnabas Publishing, 17.

[87] Harries, John. G. Campbell Morgan, *The Man and His Ministry*, Fleming Revell, 45.

ACKNOWLEDGMENTS

Special thanks to the following people who made significant contributions to this project:

Bobby Clinton—who offered counsel, encouragement and mentor sponsorship for this book and companion website. Everything I know about Bible centered leadership came from or was inspired by you.

Rebecca Jantz Johnson—who served as my content consultant. Thank you for your patience, persistence, and commitment to excellence. You caught the vision for this project and wouldn't let me settle for anything less than my best. (www.Story.Solutions)

Angeline Patrick—who serves as my personal assistant and keeps my world in order. Every person who benefits from my ministry owes a debt of gratitude to you.

Eric Hall—who handled the web development for this project. Thanks for all the after-hours communication and the spirit of partnership every step of the way.

Josiah Moore—who created the book trailer, the PDF version of the book, and provided ongoing creative consultation.

Carter Zimmerman—who refined the digital marketing process and offered ongoing creative consultation. You make everything I do better.

Dan Reiland—who stepped up on the front end of this project with tangible encouragement that pushed me over the top when it was time to launch.

Sherry Moore—who graciously traded our weekend fun to create the space for me to write.

ABOUT THE AUTHOR

As the president of nexleader, Dr. Steve Moore helps people turn increased self-awareness into effective self-leadership. His personal life mission is to inspire and equip others to live a focused life, finish well and join with God in blessing the nations. His three life passions are people development, Bible-centered leadership and world evangelization, with a special focus on developing leaders.

Steve is the creator of the Identity Profile Self-Awareness Tool (IPSAT). The IPSAT is being used by universities, organizations, local churches, and Christian coaches to help individuals discover the unique combination of their personality, strengths, skills, spiritual gifts, and passions.

From 2006 – 2015, Steve served as the president and CEO of Missio Nexus, the largest network of Great Commission oriented evangelicals in North America, representing churches, organizations and training institutions that send more than 20,000 missionaries serving in nearly every country.

Steve's ministry has taken him around the world. He has provided leadership for teams serving in Europe, Asia, Africa, South America and the Caribbean. He currently serves as board chair for World Relief, as an Executive Committee member of the board for the National Association of Evangelicals, and as Vice Chair of the Global Leadership Council for the World Evangelical Alliance Mission Commission.

Steve has written several other books, including, *The Dream Cycle: Leveraging the Power of Personal Growth, While You Were Micro-Sleeping, Who is My Neighbor? Being A Good Samaritan in a Connected World, and Seize the Vuja dé*. His e-book, *Why Dead People Make the Best Mentors: And How to Learn from Them*, is available for free from the nexleader idea portal at ideas.nexleader.com.

Steve and his wife Sherry have four adult children; they currently reside in Atlanta, Georgia.

Made in the USA
San Bernardino, CA
01 April 2018